Expanding Your Raspberry Pi

Storage, printing, peripherals,
and network connections for your
Raspberry Pi

Mark Edward Soper

Apress®

Expanding Your Raspberry Pi: Storage, printing, peripherals, and network connections for your Raspberry Pi

Mark Edward Soper
Indianapolis, Indiana, USA

ISBN-13 (pbk): 978-1-4842-2921-7
ISBN-13 (electronic): 978-1-4842-2922-4
DOI 10.1007/978-1-4842-2922-4

Library of Congress Control Number: 2017952610

Cover image designed by Freepik

Managing Director: Welmoed Spahr
Editorial Director: Todd Green
Acquisitions Editor: Aaron Black
Development Editor: James Markham
Technical Reviewer: Massimo Nardone
Coordinating Editor: Jessica Vakili
Copy Editor: Brendan Frost
Compositor: SPi Global
Indexer: SPi Global
Artist: SPi Global

Distributed to the book trade worldwide by Springer Science+Business Media New York, 233 Spring Street, 6th Floor, New York, NY 10013. Phone 1-800-SPRINGER, fax (201) 348-4505, e-mail orders-ny@springer-sbm.com, or visit www.springeronline.com. Apress Media, LLC is a California LLC and the sole member (owner) is Springer Science + Business Media Finance Inc (SSBM Finance Inc). SSBM Finance Inc is a **Delaware** corporation.

For information on translations, please e-mail rights@apress.com, or visit http://www.apress.com/rights-permissions.

Apress titles may be purchased in bulk for academic, corporate, or promotional use. eBook versions and licenses are also available for most titles. For more information, reference our Print and eBook Bulk Sales web page at http://www.apress.com/bulk-sales.

Any source code or other supplementary material referenced by the author in this book is available to readers on GitHub via the book's product page, located at www.apress.com/978-1-4842-2921-7. For more detailed information, please visit http://www.apress.com/source-code.

Printed on acid-free paper

Contents at a Glance

About the Author xiii

About the Technical Reviewer xv

Chapter 1: Raspberry Pi System Anatomy 1

Chapter 2: The Distro Bunch 17

Chapter 3: Adding Mass Storage 43

Chapter 4: Connecting to a Workgroup Network 61

Chapter 5: Sharing an Internet Connection 85

Chapter 6: Setting Up a Print and Scan Server 99

Chapter 7: Imaging and Video 123

Chapter 8: Media Serving 157

Chapter 9: GPIO Anatomy and Applications 169

Chapter 10: Taking Your Raspberry Pi on the Road 185

Index 199

Contents

About the Author xiii

About the Technical Reviewer xv

▓Chapter 1: Raspberry Pi System Anatomy 1

  Model Overview... 1

    Common Features 2

    Model A Family 3

    Model B Family 5

    Zero 9

  CPU and RAM 10

    System-on-a-Chip (SoC).. 10

    CPU, RAM, and SoC Features 11

  Ports 12

  Board-Level Connectors 13

  Integrated Network Features 13

  Power Supplies 15

  Summary.. 15

▓Chapter 2: The Distro Bunch... 17

  Raspbian 17

    Raspbian with PIXEL Fast Facts 18

    Raspbian Lite Fast Facts 20

Other Linux Distros Available with NOOBS 21

LibreELEC_R Pi 2 Overview and Fast Facts 21

Lakka_R Pi 2 Overview and Fast Facts 22

OSMC_P2 Overview and Fast Facts 23

RISC OS Overview and Fast Facts 24

Windows 10 IoT Core Overview and Fast Facts... 25

Other Linux Distros Available with PINN.. 26

Arch Linux ARM 26

RetroPie 27

Using NOOBS... 27

Installing an OS with NOOBS 27

Restarting NOOBS... 28

Using PINN: An Alternative to NOOBS 30

Using BerryBoot 33

Installing BerryBoot... 33

Installing an OS with BerryBoot.. 34

More Options for BerryBoot 37

Loading an OS with BerryBoot.. 38

Other Linux Distros for Raspberry Pi 38

FreeBSD.. 38

NetBSD 38

Fedora and CentOS.. 39

OpenWRT 39

Choosing the Best Distro for the Task 39

Creating Your Media 39

Summary.. 42

■**Chapter 3: Adding Mass Storage** **43**

Recommended Memory Card Types 43

Expanding a Partition on a Flash Memory Card 45

Determining the Current Partition Size (Parted) 46

Expanding the Partition Using Parted 47

Expanding the Partition with RootFS-Expand (CentOS) 47

Expanding the Partition Used by RISC OS 48

Connecting a USB Flash Drive or Memory Card 48

Mounting a Drive for Read/Write Access 50

Partitioning a Flash Memory Card or USB Drive 50

Formatting a Drive with ext4 File System 53

Adding and Using an External Hard Drive 53

Adding and Using a WDLabs Pi Drive 54

Wireless Drives 58

Troubleshooting 58

Incorrectly Formatted Media 58

Not Enough Power 59

Drive Can't Be Mounted in Read/Write Mode 59

Summary 59

■**Chapter 4: Connecting to a Workgroup Network** **61**

Distro and Raspberry Pi Configuration 61

Connecting to a Windows Share with PIXEL 61

Connecting to a Windows Share from the Command Line with smbclient 64

Connecting to Different Workgroups 65

Connecting to an OSX (MacOS) Share from Raspbian PIXEL 65

Using Wireless Drives 67

    Connecting to a SanDisk Connect Wireless Flash Drive 68

    Connecting to a Seagate Wireless Plus Drive 69

Printing to a Network Printer 71

    Configuring CUPS 72

    Setting Printer Defaults 74

    Testing Your Printer 75

Scanning with a Network Scanner 75

Raspberry Pi Linux Samba Server Configuration 75

    Creating Local Users 76

    Creating a Network User 77

    Configuring smb.conf 77

    Logging into the Raspberry Pi 79

Connecting to Raspberry Pi from an Android Device 80

Connecting to Raspberry Pi from an iOS Device 82

Troubleshooting 83

Summary 83

Chapter 5: Sharing an Internet Connection 85

Hardware Used in This Chapter 85

Configuring the Pi for Sharing (Hardware) 86

Configuring the Pi for Sharing (Software) 86

    Planning the Network Configuration 87

Sharing a Wired Connection Using a Wireless Adapter 89

    Sharing a Wireless Connection Using an Ethernet Port and Switch 93

Troubleshooting 98

Summary 98

Chapter 6: Setting Up a Print and Scan Server.............................. 99

Hardware Used in This Chapter.. 99

Connecting via USB.. 100

Selecting a Distro.. 100

Manual Connections to a Wireless Network.. 101

Installing and Using CUPS... 103

Adding Users to the Print Administration Group... 103

Configuring CUPS for Remote Administration.. 104

Logging into CUPS Remotely... 104

Selecting and Configuring a Printer with CUPS.. 105

Installing Printer Drivers.. 107

Installing and Configuring Samba.. 108

Connecting to a Samba Print Server with Windows.. 109

Connecting to a Samba Print Server with MacOS (OSX)....................................... 113

Installing and Configuring SANE.. 115

Configuring SANE as a Server.. 116

Connecting to SANE from Windows... 117

Connecting to SANE from MacOS (OSX)... 118

Headless Boot... 118

Connecting via SSH Using Windows.. 118

Troubleshooting.. 120

Summary.. 121

Chapter 7: Imaging and Video.. 123

Hardware Used in This Chapter.. 123

Connecting a Camera to the Camera Port.. 123

Swapping Cables for a Raspberry Pi Zero.. 125

Enabling the Camera Port.. 127

Using Raspivid to Capture Video 129

    Raspivid Options and Examples 129

    Playing Videos with OMXplayer 132

    Converting Recordings with MP4Box 132

Using Raspistill to Take Photos 133

    Taking Time-Lapse Photos with Raspistill 134

    Viewing Raspistill Photo Metadata 135

Controlling the Raspberry Pi Camera with Python 136

Controlling Your Raspberry Pi Camera with Android or iOS 138

    Using RaspiCAM Remote for Android 138

    Using BerryCam for iOS 140

Using a Webcam with a Raspberry Pi 143

    Using Fswebcam 143

    Capturing Video or Stills Using Guvcview 144

    Using RaspiCAM Remote with a Webcam 145

Connecting to an Image Scanner 146

    Installing SANE with PIXEL, Other Linux GUIs 147

    Using Simple Scan 148

    Using Xscan 150

Troubleshooting 153

    Raspberry Pi Camera Issues 153

    Camera App Issues 154

    Network Issues 154

    Webcam Issues 154

    Scanner Issues 154

Summary 155

Chapter 8: Media Serving **157**

Hardware Used in This Chapter 157

Selecting a Distro 157

BerryBoot, WD PiDrive, and Media Serving 158

Using LibreELEC 161

    Adding Media Files 163

Connecting to a PLEX Server with RasPlex 166

Troubleshooting 168

    Network Settings 168

    Audio Playback 168

Summary 168

Chapter 9: GPIO Anatomy and Applications **169**

Hardware Used in This Chapter 169

    What Can You Do with GPIO? 169

    GPIO Pinouts 170

    Raspberry Pi GPIO Pin Numbering Schemes 171

Programming the GPIO Interface 173

Using a Gertboard 173

Using a PiFace Control and Display Board 175

Using a Breadboard 178

Troubleshooting 183

Summary 183

Chapter 10: Taking Your Raspberry Pi on the Road **185**

Power Usage 185

Configuring the Raspberry Pi for Minimal Power Consumption 186

    Disabling HDMI 187

    Disabling Onboard LEDs 187

Enabling Login and Control via TTY 188

Disabling USB Hub and Ethernet 190

Choosing a Power Source 191

Estimated Battery Runtimes.. 191

Car Chargers and Raspberry Pi 193

Using Intelligent Power Management Peripherals 194

MoPi Mobile Power for Raspberry Pi.. 194

LiFePO$_4$wered/Pi 3 195

Sleepy Pi and Sleepy Pi 2 196

Comparing Power Management Products for Raspberry Pi.............. 197

Troubleshooting... 197

Summary... 198

Index... 199

About the Author

Mark Edward Soper is an internationally published expert on technical topics ranging from CompTIA A+ Certification to Microsoft Windows and an instructor who has taught thousands of students in industry seminars and employee training about computer and device troubleshooting and repair, digital imaging, Microsoft Windows, and networking. Mark has seen the industry change from an emphasis on understanding hardware and what makes it work to the computer as appliance. He's excited to see that devices such as the Raspberry Pi are not only useful for teaching how computers work but also capable of being put to work in home and business environments. Mark thanks God for the opportunity to share technical knowledge around the world and for his family, who use technology at work and play.

About the Technical Reviewer

Massimo Nardone has more than 22 years of experience in Security, Web/Mobile development, Cloud, and IT Architecture. His true IT passions are Security and Android.

He has been programming and teaching how to program with Android, Perl, PHP, Java, VB, Python, C/C++, and MySQL for more than 20 years.

He holds a Master of Science degree in Computing Science from the University of Salerno, Italy.

He has worked as a Project Manager, Software Engineer, Research Engineer, Chief Security Architect, Information Security Manager, PCI/SCADA Auditor, and Senior Lead IT Security/Cloud/SCADA Architect for many years.

Technical skills include: Security, Android, Cloud, Java, MySQL, Drupal, Cobol, Perl, Web and Mobile development, MongoDB, D3, Joomla, Couchbase, C/C++, WebGL, Python, Pro Rails, Django CMS, Jekyll, Scratch, etc.

He currently works as Chief Information Security Officer (CISO) for Cargotec Oyj.

He worked as visiting lecturer and supervisor for exercises at the Networking Laboratory of the Helsinki University of Technology (Aalto University). He holds four international patents (PKI, SIP, SAML, and Proxy areas).

Massimo has reviewed more than 40 IT books for different publishing companies, and he is the coauthor of *Pro Android Games* (Apress, 2015).

This book is dedicated to Antti Jalonen and his family, who are always there when I need them.

CHAPTER 1

Raspberry Pi System Anatomy

Raspberry Pi is a family of low-cost single-board computers originally designed for computer and electronics education. The combination of low cost, flexibility, and widespread operating systems support has made the Raspberry Pi family one of the leading computer platforms for hobbyists as well as educators. IT professionals are also taking a closer look at the Raspberry Pi as a platform for the Internet of Things (IoT), thanks to the introduction of a Windows 10 edition that supports the Raspberry Pi 3.

In this chapter, we'll introduce you to the members of the family to help you find the best model for your needs.

Model Overview

Current models of the Raspberry Pi include the following:

- Pi 1 Model A+
- Pi 2 Model B
- Pi 3 Model B
- Pi Zero

© Mark Edward Soper 2017
M. E. Soper, *Expanding Your Raspberry Pi*, DOI 10.1007/978-1-4842-2922-4_1

These are shown in Figure 1-1, along with the older Pi 1 Model B.

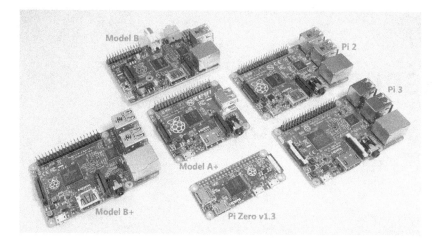

Figure 1-1. *Raspberry Pi Model B, Model B+, Model A+, Pi 2, Pi 3, and Pi Zero*

Common Features

All Pi models have these common features:

- ARM architecture

- Broadcom BCM28xx series SoC (System-on-a-Chip)

- At least one USB 2.0 port

- HDMI video output

- SD-family memory card slot

- GPIO (General-Purpose Input/Output) connector

Beyond these common features, there are plenty of differences to keep in mind as you work to select the best model for your needs.

■ **Note** GPIO pins have user-defined functions. The GPIO connector on Raspberry Pi includes pins for GPIO, power, ground, and other functions. See the pinouts in Chapter 9 for details.

Model A vs. Model B Boards

Raspberry Pi Model A boards have limited expandability, slower processors, and less RAM than comparable Model B boards. See the following sections for details.

Model A Family

Model A boards can be distinguished from later models by their lack of an Ethernet port and the inclusion of only one USB port. They use 32-bit single-core 700MHz processors.

Model A

The original Model A board (not shown) features a 26-pin GPIO bus, a single standard-size SD card slot, and both composite analog and HDMI digital video output.

Model A+

Model A boards have largely been replaced by Model A+ boards, which use the same 40-pin GPIO connector as Model B boards. The Model A+ board was the smallest Raspberry Pi board until the introduction of the Raspberry Pi Zero. The Model A+ board remains the smallest board to have a 40-pin GPIO connector, as the Pi Zero has open GPIO solder holes rather than a connector. Model A+ is pictured in Figures 1-2, 1-3, and 1-4.

Figure 1-2. Raspberry Pi Model A+'s camera port, audio port, and USB port

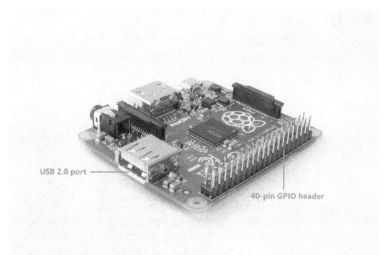

Figure 1-3. *Raspberry Pi Model A+ USB port and 40-pin GPIO connector*

Figure 1-4. *Raspberry Pi Model A+'s serial display interface (SDI), Micro-USB power connector, and HDMI video port. The microSD card slot is beneath the display connector.*

Model B Family

The Model B family includes more expandability than the Model A family because it features more USB ports and an Ethernet port. Model B boards represent three generations of Raspberry Pi:

- First generation (B, B+)

- Second generation (Pi 2)

- Third generation (Pi 3)

Model B (First Generation)

The original Model B board (see Figures 1-5 and 1-6) was the first Raspberry Pi board to include two USB 2.0 ports and a 10/100 Ethernet port. It also featured the same combination of HDMI A/V, audio, composite video ports, 26-pin GPIO connector, and full-size SD card slot as found on the Model A.

Figure 1-5. *Raspberry Pi Model B's HDMI port, Ethernet port, and dual USB 2.0 ports*

5

Figure 1-6. *Raspberry Pi Model B's stereo audio port, composite video port, 26-pin GPIO connector, serial display interface (SDI), and Micro-USB power connector. The SD card slot is beneath the display connector.*

Model B+, Pi 2, and Pi 3

Currently, Model B computers are available as improved first-generation (B+), second-generation (Pi 2), or third-generation (Pi 3) models. These boards feature

- 40-pin GPIO connector

- Four USB 2.0 ports

- 10/100 Ethernet port

- microSD card slot

B+ boards use the same single-core 700MHz ARM processor used by Model A and A+ boards.

The original Pi 2 uses a 900MHz quad-core 32-bit processor. Pi 2 v1.2 also includes a 900MHz quad-core processor, but one which also supports 64-bit operating systems.

From the top, Pi 3 looks almost identical to Pi 2 v1.1 and Pi 2 v1.2, but includes Pi's first 1.2GHz 64-bit processor. It's easier to distinguish these boards from each other from the bottom. Figures 1-7 and 1-8 illustrate the top and bottom views of these boards.

Figure 1-7. *Top view of Raspberry Pi B+ (left), Pi 2 (center), and Pi 3 (right)*

Figure 1-8. *Bottom view of Raspberry Pi B+ (left), Pi 2 (center), and Pi 3 (right)*

Figures 1-9 and 1-10 provide a closer look at the Pi 3. The features called out in these figures are also present on Pi Model B+ and Pi 2.

Figure 1-9. *Raspberry Pi 3's GPIO header, display header, Micro-USB power connector, HDMI audio/video port, camera header, and stereo audio port*

Figure 1-10. *Raspberry Pi 3's 10/100 Ethernet port and quartet of USB 2.0 ports*

Zero

Pi Zero (Figures 1-11 and 1-12) is the smallest, thinnest, and least-expensive member of the Raspberry Pi family. It is so inexpensive ($5.00 US as this book goes to press) that some magazines devoted to Raspberry Pi sold special issues with a Pi Zero board attached to the front cover when Pi Zero was introduced.

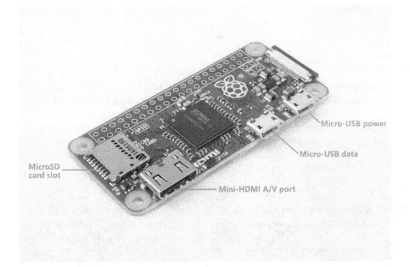

Figure 1-11. *Raspberry Pi Zero's top-mounted microSD slot, Mini-HDMI video port, and Micro-USB data and power ports*

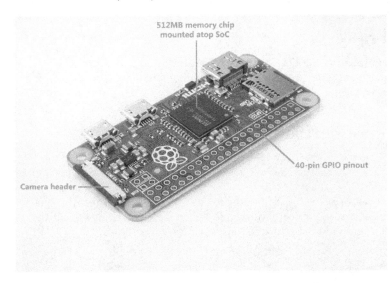

Figure 1-12. *Raspberry Pi Zero's camera port and 40-hole GPIO pinout*

Like other recent Pi models, Pi Zero includes a microSD slot, but it is top-mounted, rather than bottom-mounted as with other Pi models. Pi Zero also includes a Mini-HDMI port, a Micro-USB (USB-on-the-Go) data port, and the same Micro-USB power port used by earlier Pi models.

Pi Zero has the same 40-pin GPIO pinout as Model B boards, but instead of a connector, the holes are open for temporary or soldered connections.

Pi Zero has no onboard network connections. All network connections must be made via the Micro-USB port.

v1.2 vs. v.1.3

Pi Zero was originally introduced without a camera connector. This version is known as v1.2. Version 1.3, the current version (shown in Figures 1-11 and 1-12), adds a camera connector to the opposite end of the board from the microSD card slot.

Pi Zero v1.3's camera connector is electronically compatible with the cameras available for other Pi versions. However, it uses a different cable. Users can replace the original cable with a Pi Zero cable.

Pi Zero W

Pi Zero W is based on Pi Zero v1.3, but also includes the same wireless radio chip (Wi-Fi and Bluetooth) used on the Pi 3. It was introduced in early 2017 and has a US retail price of $10.00.

 Note   To learn more about using the Raspberry Pi camera and connecting the camera to different Raspberry Pi models, see Chapter 7.

CPU and RAM

Although most Raspberry Pi Model B boards look very much alike, there are major differences in processor cores, processor speed, 32-bit vs. 64-bit support, RAM size, and RAM speed between all Raspberry Pi models.

System-on-a-Chip (SoC)

All Raspberry Pi models use SoC technology, which combines CPU, video, and other features normally found on separate chips into a single piece of silicon. On boards with 256MB or 512MB of RAM, the RAM chip is stacked above the SoC and the SoC and RAM are installed as a single subassembly. On boards with 1GB of RAM, the RAM chip is attached to the bottom of the board with connection to the SoC running through the board. This results in a sandwich with three layers as viewed from the top:

- SoC
- Raspberry Pi board
- RAM

Users must replace their boards to obtain faster CPU or RAM performance. Fortunately, Raspberry Pi boards are inexpensive.

Raspberry Pi boards use Broadcom BCM28xx SoC chips with different processor cores and amounts of RAM onboard, depending upon the board or revision level.

CPU, RAM, and SoC Features

Raspberry Pi Model A (1, 1+) and Model B (1, 1+) use the 700MHz version of the ARM1176JZF-S CPU. Raspberry Pi Zero and Zero W use the 1GHz version. This is a single-core CPU that supports the ARMv6Z 32-bit architecture. These boards use the Broadcom BCM2835 SoC. The memory is mounted atop the SoC chip on these boards.

Raspberry Pi 2 has a big upgrade in performance with a 900MHz quad-core ARMv7 Cortex-A7 CPU incorporated into the Broadcom BCM2836 SoC.

Raspberry Pi 3 breaks the 1GHz barrier with a 64-bit ARMv8 Cortex-A53 CPU incorporated into the Broadcom BCM2837 SoC.

In Raspberry Pi 2 and Pi 3, the RAM is located on the bottom of the board, rather than connected on top of the SoC as with other models.

■ **Note**   For more information about the ARM1176JZF-S, see www.arm.com/products/ processors/classic/arm11/arm1176.php. Learn more about the Cortex A7 processor at www.arm.com/products/processors/cortex-a/cortex-a7.php. Dig deeper into the Cortex A53 processor at www.arm.com/products/processors/cortex-a/cortex-a53-processor.php.

Table 1-1 outlines the CPU, RAM, and SoC used by Raspberry Pi boards.

Table 1-1. *Raspberry Pi SoC, CPU, and RAM*

Pi Model	SoC	CPU (Cores)	Speed	RAM
A	BCM2835	ARM1176JZF-S (1)	700MHz	256MB
A+	BCM2835	ARM1176JZF-S (1)	700MHz	256MB/512MB*
B	BCM2835	ARM1176JZF-S (1)	700MHz	256MB/512MB*
B+	BCM2835	ARM1176JZF-S (1)	700MHz	256MB/512MB*
2	BCM2836	ARM Cortex-A7 (4)	900MHz	1GB
2 v1.2	BCM2836	ARM Cortex-A53 (4)	900MHz	1GB
3	BCM2837	ARM Cortex-A53 (4)	1.2GHz	1GB
Zero 1.2, 1.3, and W	BCM2835	ARM1176JZF-S (1)	1GHz	512MB

Original production included 256MB of RAM. Models produced starting in May 2016 include 512MB of RAM.

Ports

The ports included in full-size Raspberry Pi models include

- USB 2.0
- HDMI v1.3
- Audio out
- 10/100 Ethernet*
- Micro-USB power port

*Not included in Raspberry Pi Model A or A+.
The ports included in Raspberry Pi Zero models include

- Micro-USB 2.0 data port
- Micro-USB power port
- Mini-HDMI v1.3

Table 1-2 summarizes port types on the different Raspberry Pi models and versions.

Table 1-2. *Raspberry Pi Port Types and Quantities*

Pi Model	# of USB 2.0	Ethernet	HDMI	Audio Out
A	1	N/A	1	Yes
A+	1	N/A	1	Yes
B	2	10/100 (1)	1	Yes
B+	4	10/100 (1)	1	Yes
2 (v1.1, 1.2)	4	10/100 (1)	1	Yes
3	4	10/100 (1)	1	Yes
Zero (v1.2, 1.3)	1*	N/A	1**	N/A

*Micro-USB
**Mini-HDMI

■ **Note**   Raspberry Pi Model A and Model B have a separate composite video interface. Raspberry Pi Model A+, B+, 2, and 3 combine the composite video interface with the 3.5mm analog audio jack. Audio is the default usage. To switch from the default HDMI video output to composite video on these models, see Chapter 2.

Board-Level Connectors

Board-level connectors included in Raspberry Pi models include

- Camera interface (CSI)

- Display interface (DSI)

- GPIO connector (all except Raspberry Pi Zero, Zero W) or GPIO pinout with open holes (Raspberry Pi Zero, Zero W)

- SD card or microSD card

The CSI is used by the Raspberry Pi camera, available in 5MP or 8MP versions (see Chapter 7 for details).

The DSI is used by various display devices, including the PiFace (see Chapter 9 for details).

Original Model A and Model B Raspberry Pi models support SD or SDHC memory cards. Model B+, Pi 2, Pi 3, and Pi Zero support microSD or microSDHC memory cards. For SDXC cards, see the following Note.

■ **Note**   It is also possible to use 64GB SDXC or microSDXC memory cards with Raspberry Pi models by reformatting the card using the FAT32 file system (64GB and larger cards use the ExFAT/FAT64 file system by default). Linux and MacOS (OSX) can format SDXC cards using FAT32 by deleting the original partition and reformatting the card. With Windows, you can use SD Formatter and FAT32 Format to create a FAT32 partition that uses the entire card. For details, see Chapter 2.

Integrated Network Features

When networking is considered, Raspberry Pi boards can be divided into three categories:

- Boards without integrated networking

- Boards with integrated wired networking

- Boards with integrated wireless networking

Raspberry Pi Model A, A+, and Zero do not include any onboard networking. A USB wireless adapter or a USB wired Ethernet adapter can be used with these boards. To use more than one USB device at the same time, a USB 2.0 hub must be used (Figures 1-13, 1-14).

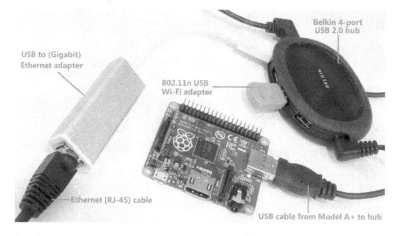

Figure 1-13. *Raspberry Pi A+ is using a Belkin 4-port USB hub to connect to a USB Wi-Fi adapter and a USB Ethernet adapter*

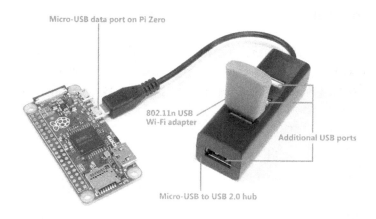

Figure 1-14. *A Raspberry Pi Zero v1.3 is using a four-port Micro-USB hub to connect to a USB Wi-Fi adapter*

Raspberry Pi B, B+, Pi 2, and Pi 3 all include a 10/100 Ethernet port (refer to Figures 1-5, 1-10).

Raspberry Pi 3 includes both wired (10/100 Ethernet) and wireless (802.11n and Bluetooth 4.1/LE) support. A close look at the Raspberry Pi 3 compared to a Raspberry Pi 2 reveals the tiny radio chip and antenna (Figure 1-15). The Pi Zero W uses the same radio chip and antenna as the Pi 3.

Figure 1-15. *The Raspberry Pi 3's underside contains the radio chip, and the top of the board has a surface-mounted antenna in place of the power and activity lights of the Raspberry Pi 2. On the Pi 3, the power and activity lights are located on the right edge of the board near the round case mounting hole.*

Power Supplies

At a minimum, any full-size Raspberry Pi should use a 2.0A power supply. However, a 2.5A power supply is recommended for greater reliability, especially if the Pi's SPI, camera interface, or GPIO pins will be used.

Summary

The Raspberry Pi 3 provides the most powerful combination of features of all Raspberry Pi models. As you will learn in detail in Chapter 2, it is one of two Raspberry Pi models suitable for use with Windows 10 IoT Core (the other being the Raspberry Pi 2).

If you need Linux compatibility, any of the Raspberry Pi boards will work, but the limited RAM in the original Model A, Model B, and early-production Model B+ make these boards better options for appliance (single-task) or command-line Linux releases. Look for 512MB or 1GB boards if you want to run a GUI.

In Chapter 2, you will learn about Linux and Windows versions made for Raspberry Pi. Choosing the right operating system to work with your Raspberry Pi is the next step in expanding it.

■ ■ ■

## CHAPTER 2

The Distro Bunch

The Raspberry Pi family of single-board computers has broad operating systems support in both Linux and non-Linux environments. Your first step in expanding your Raspberry Pi is choosing the right distro or operating system for the job (or jobs) you want to perform with your Raspberry Pi.

In this chapter, you'll take a tour of the major Linux distros and other operating systems available for Raspberry Pi. You'll learn what they include, what tasks they're designed to perform, what they look like, and the specific Raspberry Pi versions they support. Whether you use a diminutive Raspberry Pi Zero, the highest-performance Raspberry Pi 3 Model B, or another option, you'll find several choices to consider.

This chapter also covers installation methods, including the use of NOOBS and alternatives such as BerryBoot and PIIN.

Raspbian

Most Raspberry Pi boards (with the exception of the Raspberry Pi Zero and Zero W) are bundled with Raspbian, a Linux distro that is based on Debian. Raspbian is officially supported by the Raspberry Pi foundation; you can download the latest version of Raspbian for all Pi versions from the foundation's web site.

Raspbian is available in two forms: Raspbian Jessie with Pixel includes the PIXEL desktop, and Raspbian Jessie Lite is a minimal version. Both are available through the NOOBS installer included on the Raspberry Pi flash drive included with most Raspberry Pi boards.

Note   To learn more about using NOOBS, see "Using NOOBS," in this chapter.

Raspbian with PIXEL includes several programming languages and tools, making it a good choice for a ready-to-use programming environment. It also includes LibreOFFICE, a web browser, e-mail, and other office apps.

Raspbian Lite boots to a command line. It's fully customizable; you can add your choice of GUI, languages, web browser, and so on. If you're new to Linux, be prepared for a long slog.

© Mark Edward Soper 2017

M. E. Soper, *Expanding Your Raspberry Pi*, DOI 10.1007/978-1-4842-2922-4_2

■ **Note**   For a step-by-step tutorial on creating a customized Raspbian Lite configuration with your choice of GUI, icons, and more, see the article **[GUIDE]Raspbian Lite with PIXEL/LXDE/XFCE/MATE/Openbox GUI** in the Raspberry Pi forum (`www.raspberrypi.org/forums/viewtopic.php?f=66&t=133691`).

Raspbian with PIXEL Fast Facts

Here's a quick summary of Raspbian with PIXEL.

- **Web site:** `www.raspberrypi.org/downloads/raspbian/`

- **Recommended uses:** programming, office applications, Python games, Minecraft

- **Raspberry Pi versions supported:** all

- **How to install:** via NOOBS, BerryBoot, or PINN; command line (Linux, OSX); Win32DiskImager (Windows)

■ **Tip**   Whether you install Raspbian with PIXEL or Raspbian Lite, use these two commands first from the command prompt (Lite) or from a terminal session (PIXEL) to assure you have the most up-to-date Raspbian OS files:

```
sudo apt-get update
sudo apt-get dist-upgrade
```

Figures 2-1 and 2-2 illustrate the PIXEL desktop and some of the installed apps and tools.

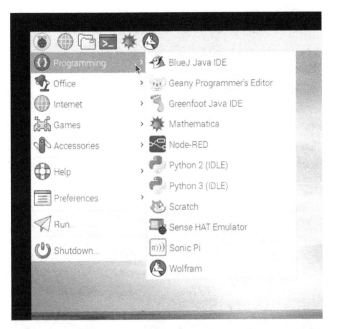

Figure 2-1. *Programming tools and languages included with Raspbian's PIXEL desktop*

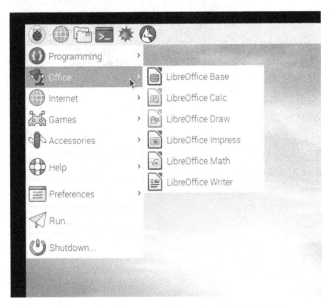

Figure 2-2. *Raspbian's PIXEL desktop includes LibreOffice*

Raspbian Lite Fast Facts

Here's a quick summary of Raspbian Lite.

- **Web site:** www.raspberrypi.org/downloads/raspbian/

- **Recommended uses:** command-line Linux, headless operation, great for DIY customization

- **Raspberry Pi versions supported:** all

- **How to install:** via NOOBS, BerryBoot, or PINN; command line (Linux, OSX); Win32DiskImager (Windows)

The default command-line interface for Raspbian Lite and the raspi-config configuration utility window are shown in Figure 2-3.

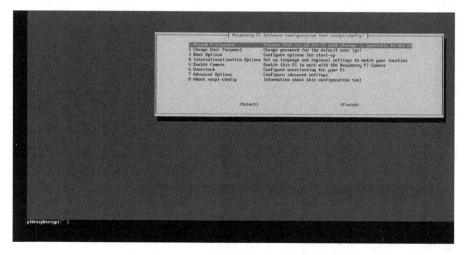

Figure 2-3. *A few configuration options are available through the raspi-config utility, but most changes to your system must be applied via the command line*

■ **Note**   By default, Raspbian Lite requires the user to log in. The default username is **pi** and the password is **raspberry**. If you prefer to log in automatically, use raspi-config to change this option. For other default passwords, see www.raspberry-pi-geek.com/howto/Passwords.

Other Linux Distros Available with NOOBS

The following Linux distros can be installed using NOOBS, the boot manager included with most Raspberry Pi boards.

LibreELEC_R Pi 2 Overview and Fast Facts

LibreELEC_R Pi 2, unlike Raspbian, is a single-purpose distro, made especially for entertainment and media serving. As Figure 2-4 illustrates, it is a Raspberry Pi version of the KODI open source media player.

- **Web site:** http://libreelec.tv

- **Recommended uses:** entertainment and media serving (based on Kodi)

- **Raspberry Pi versions supported:** Pi 2, Pi 3

- **How to install:** via NOOBS, BerryBoot, or PINN; LibreELEC USB-SD Creator (available for Windows, OSX, and Linux)

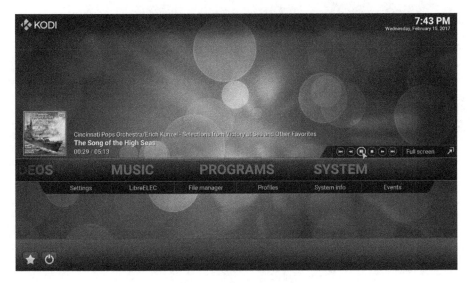

Figure 2-4. Playing an album track through Libre-ELEC

Lakka_R Pi 2 Overview and Fast Facts

Lakka is based on RetroArch Linux, a popular Linux distro used for retro gameplay. Lakka can be used with a wide variety of ROMs and game images and contains emulation cores for classic 8-bit and 16-bit consoles as well as DOSBOX and other IBM gaming environments.

- **Web site:** www.lakka.tv

- **Recommended uses:** retro gaming emulation

- **Raspberry Pi versions supported:** Pi 2, Pi 3 (older Pi versions also supported with separate download)

- **How to install:** via NOOBS, BerryBoot, or PINN; command line (Linux, OSX); Win32DiskImager (Windows)

Figures 2-5 and 2-6 illustrate the Lakka_R Pi 2 configuration menu.

Figure 2-5. *The Lakka-R Pi 2 main menu*

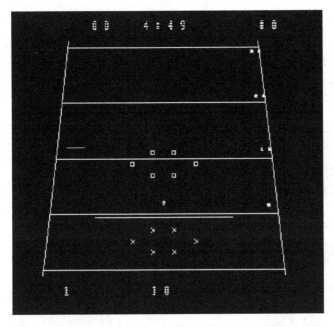

Figure 2-6. *Playing Vectrex Blitz with Lakka-R Pi 2*

OSMC_P2 Overview and Fast Facts

OSMC_P2 is also based on KODI, but differs mainly in its user interface. OSMC_P2 provides a very clean and easy-to-use configuration dialog (Figure 2-7).

- **Web site:** https://osmc.tv
- **Recommended uses:** open source media center
- **Raspberry Pi versions supported:** Pi 2, Pi 3
- **How to install:** via NOOBS, BerryBoot, or PINN; downloadable installer for Windows, OSX, and Linux

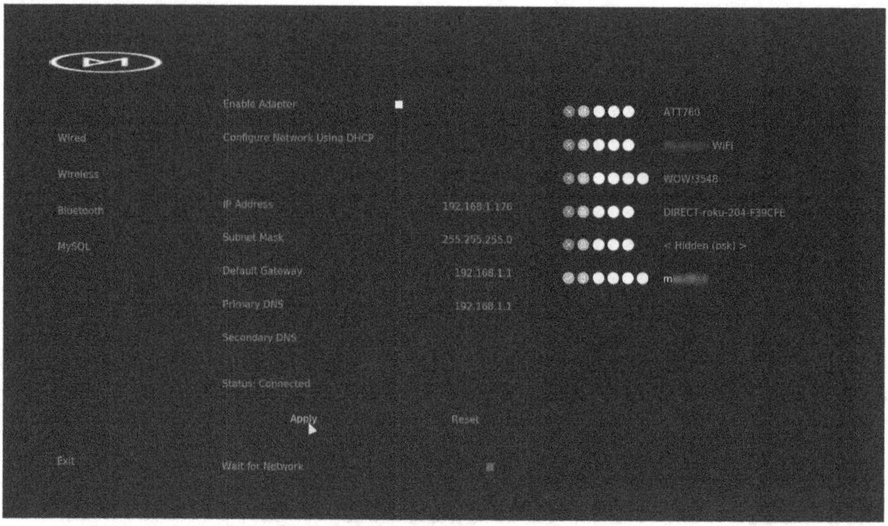

Figure 2-7. *Configuring the wireless network with OSMC_P2*

RISC OS Overview and Fast Facts

RISC OS may look like Linux, but it isn't. It's actually the latest version of Arthur. Arthur dates back to 1987, when it was first developed for the Acorn Archimedes. Unlike Linux distros, Windows, or OSX, RISC OS puts the scroll wheel (which is also a button) on typical mice to work. For example, to close down a RISC OS session, you can use the middle button/wheel to click the Raspberry Pi icon in the lower right-hand corner and select Shutdown (or use Ctrl-Shift-F12).

- **Web site:** www.riscosopen.org/content/

- **Recommended uses:** for programming in BBC BASIC, experimenting with a non-Linux OS

- **Raspberry Pi versions supported:** Pi Model A, B, A+, B, 2 (for Pi 3, install updated Beta RPi ROM with a date of 2017 or newer)

- **How to install:** via NOOBS, BerryBoot, or PINN; command line (Linux, OSX); Win32DiskImager (Windows)

▪ **Note**   Because RISC OS is not based on Linux, use the RISC Open Org web site as the recommended app source. For a list of apps included in RISC OS, see www.riscosopen.org/ wiki/documentation/show/Software%20information. The Nut Pi apps package provides a cost-effective and easy way to add more options. It's available from www.riscosopen.org/content/sales/nutpi.

Figure 2-8 illustrates the RISC OS desktop.

Figure 2-8. *A portion of the RISC OS desktop with open Resources/Apps and Configuration windows*

Windows 10 IoT Core Overview and Fast Facts

Windows 10 IoT (Internet of Things) Core, like RISC OS, isn't a Linux distro. However, unlike any other operating system that can be installed using NOOBS, Windows 10 IoT Core isn't a stand-alone OS. It's designed to be controlled and configured by a computer running Windows 10 that is running the Windows 10 IoT Core Dashboard. Users can create apps in C#, C++, or Python using the free Visual Studio Community app and send them to the Raspberry Pi for execution. Apps can control the Raspberry Pi by itself or to devices connected to the Raspberry Pi.

- **Web site:** https://developer.microsoft.com/en-us/windows/iot

- **Recommended uses:** for building projects and apps; use in conjunction with a PC running Windows 10

- **Raspberry Pi versions supported:** Pi 2, Pi 3

- **How to install:** via NOOBS, BerryBoot, or PINN; command line (Linux, OSX); Win32DiskImager (Windows); from Windows 10 IoT on PC (Figure 2-9)

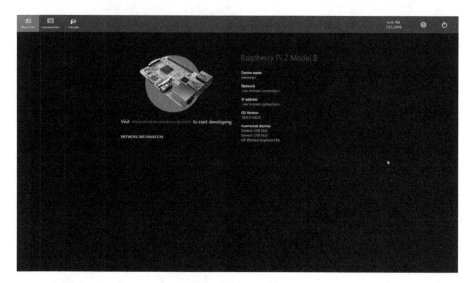

Figure 2-9. A Raspberry Pi 2 running Windows 10 IoT Core

Other Linux Distros Available with PINN

The following Linux distros can be installed using PINN, an alternative to NOOBS available from Source Forge.

Arch Linux ARM

Arch Linux ARM provides the classic Linux terminal interface, using pacman as the package manager. Choose Arch Linux ARM if you want to build a completely customized Linux environment from scratch. When installed from PINN, choose Arch 2 for R Pi 2 or Arch64 for R Pi 3. The initial Arch Linux installation is very fast because, unlike most Linux distros for Raspberry Pi, Arch Linux includes hardly any packages. It's up to you to decide what to add and install what you want.

- **Web site:** https://archlinuxarm.org/

- **Recommended uses:** full customization of Linux from terminal to a variety of GUIs

- **Raspberry Pi versions supported:** all*

- **How to install:** via PINN or Berryblue; command line (Linux, OSX); Win32DiskImager (Windows).

    *Download images available from https://sourceforge. net/projects/archlinux-rpi2/ (for R Pi 2, 3) or https:// sourceforge.net/projects/archlinuxrpi/ (for R Pi Zero, 1, 1+)

RetroPie

RetroPie is a classic game emulator that has support for games from Atari 2600 and Intellivison to Playstation 2, IBM PC, and arcade consoles. You can use it with a gamepad or keyboard.

- **Web site:** https://retropie.org.uk/

- **Recommended uses:** game emulator

- **Raspberry Pi versions supported:** all (R Pi 3 recommended)

- **How to install:** via PINN or BerryBoot; command line (Linux, OSX); Win32DiskImager (Windows); Apple Pi Baker (OSX); Etcher (Linux, OSX, Windows)

Using NOOBS

NOOBS is short for "New Out of Box Setup," and is provided on the microSD card included with most Raspberry Pi boards. It can also be downloaded from www.raspberrypi.org/downloads/noobs/. NOOBS makes installing supported operating systems very simple.

Note NOOBS is available in two forms: NOOBS, which contains Raspbian, or NOOBS Lite, which does not include any operating system. To learn how to create a bootable copy of NOOBS, see "Creating Your Media," in this chapter.

Installing an OS with NOOBS

To install an OS with NOOBS:

1. Insert the NOOBS flash card into the Raspberry Pi.

2. Connect power to the Raspberry Pi.

3. To install Raspbian from NOOBS, click the empty check box and click the **Install** icon.

4. To install another OS (or to install any OS with NOOBS Lite), you must have an Internet connection. If a wired connection is not present, but a supported Wi-Fi connection is available, click the **Wifi Networks** icon.

5. Select a network, and enter the password. Click the **OK** button.

6. The default language is English (UK). Use the menu at the bottom of the screen to choose the language desired and to change the keyboard setting.

7. To install any listed OS, click its empty check box and click the
    Install icon (Figure 2-10).

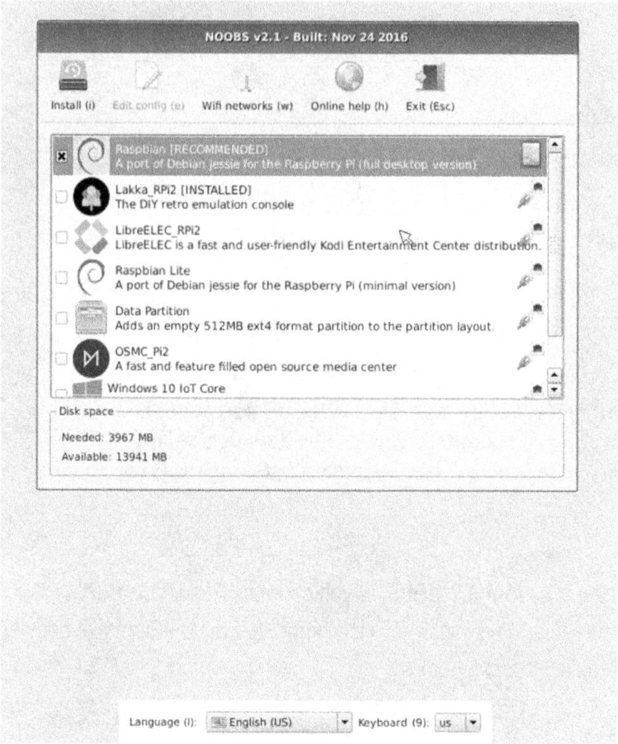

Figure 2-10. *Preparing to install Raspbian with NOOBS*

8. The OS is downloaded and installed. A progress bar informs
    you of the installation steps.

9. Click **OK** when finished. The system reboots and your select
    OS launches.

Restarting NOOBS

One significant advantage of installing supported operating systems with NOOBS over
creating a dedicated flash card for an OS is the ability to reboot the system, restart
NOOBS, and install a different operating system on the same media. This does not create
a multiboot environment, but makes experimenting easier than if you needed to create
a unique flash memory card for each OS. To return to NOOBS, start the Raspberry Pi and
watch for the recovery mode prompt shown in Figure 2-11. Hold down either Shift key
until the NOOBS menu (refer to Figure 2-10) appears.

Figure 2-11. *The recovery mode prompt. Hold down the Shift key to restart NOOBS*

■ **Note** PINN uses the same recovery mode prompt as NOOBS to return to the OS installation or configuration menu. See "Using PINN: An Alternative to NOOBS," in this chapter for more about PINN.

From the NOOBS OS menu, you can also select the installed operating system and change its startup options:

1. Click the empty check box for the installed OS.

2. Click **Edit config**.

3. Click the appropriate tab.

4. Make the changes needed in config.txt or other configuration files (Figure 2-12).

Figure 2-12. Editing the config.txt configuration file for Raspbian (already installed)

5. Click **OK** when finished.

Using PINN: An Alternative to NOOBS

PINN (PINN is not NOOBS) is an enhanced alternative to NOOBS. Get PINN (technically, Pinn-Lite, because it is not bundled with an OS), from `https://sourceforge.net/projects/pinn/files/`.

◼ **Note** To learn how to create a bootable copy of PINN, see "Creating Your Media," in this chapter.

PINN's main menu (Figure 2-13) is very similar to NOOBS, but it includes operating systems not currently available through NOOBS (Arch 2, Arch 64, and RetroPie2). As with NOOBS Lite, you must have a network connection to select and download an OS.

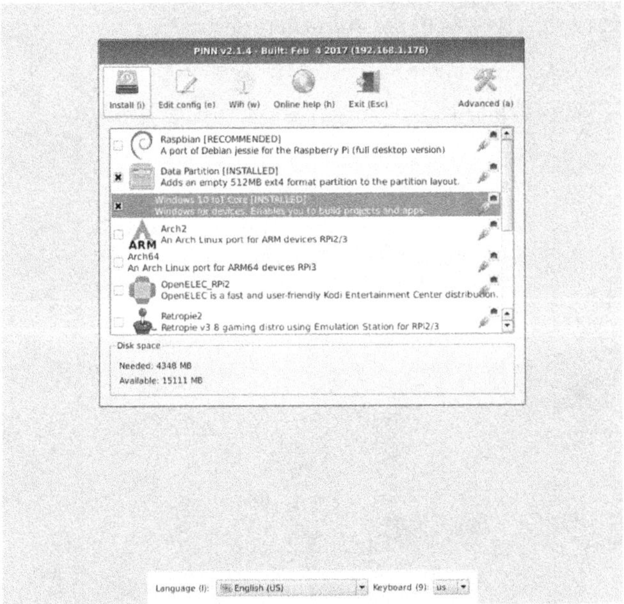

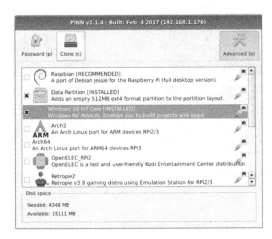

Figure 2-13. *PINN's main menu*

Click the Advanced icon to see the options to clone the PINN flash memory card or to password-protect the installed operating system (Figure 2-14).

Figure 2-14. *PINN's Advanced menu*

Here's how to use the Clone option:

1. Make sure the Raspberry Pi is disconnected from power.

2. Connect a USB card reader to the Raspberry Pi.

3. Insert a microSD card (at least 8GB) into the card reader.

4. Insert a PINN microSD card into the Raspberry Pi.

5. Connect the Raspberry Pi to power.

6. After PINN boots, click the **Advanced** icon.

7. Click the **Clone** icon.

8. Make sure that the Copy From Device is the Internal SD card and that the Copy To Device is the card reader (Figure 2-15).

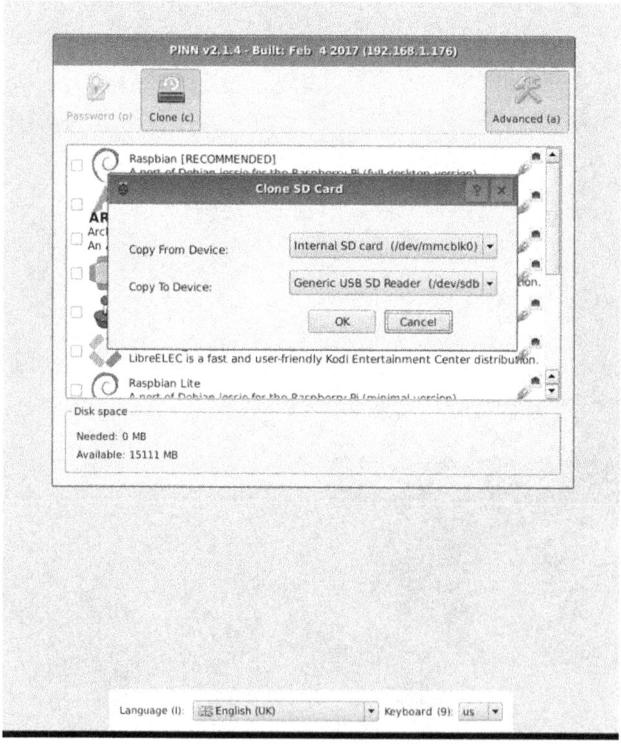

Figure 2-15. Preparing to clone the PINN card

9. Click **OK** to continue.

10. Click **Yes** to confirm the operation.

11. Click **OK** on the Clone Completed message. The card in the card reader now has a copy of the PINN memory card and any installed operating system.

Using BerryBoot

BerryBoot (`www.berryterminal.com`) takes a different approach than NOOBS or PINN to make OS installation easier. Unlike NOOBS and PINN, BerryBoot supports installing operating system images from USB flash drives, installing operating systems to a drive separate from the boot drive, and supports multibooting from a single microSD card.

■ **Note** To learn how to create a bootable copy of BerryBoot, see "Creating Your Media," in this chapter.

Installing BerryBoot

After booting your Raspberry Pi with BerryBoot, the Welcome configuration dialog appears (Figure 2-16). Select the appropriate settings for overscan, network connection (if Wifi is selected, you will be prompted to select a network and log into it), audio, timezone, and keyboard location. Click **OK** to continue.

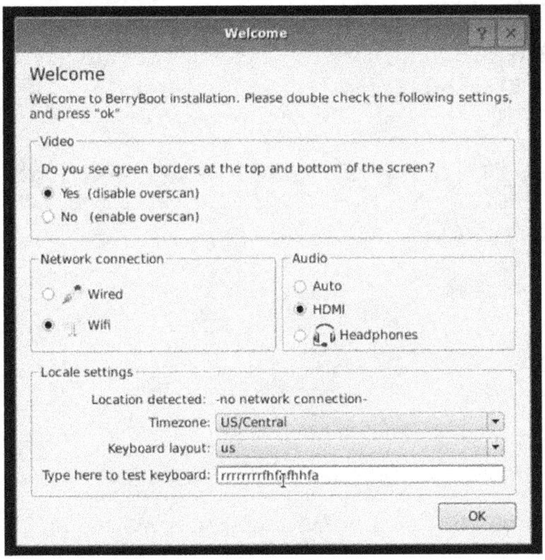

Figure 2-16. Initial BerryBoot configuration

To install BerryBoot to the boot drive, select the first drive listed. To install BerryBoot to a different drive, insert the appropriate media, then select the drive (Figure 2-17).

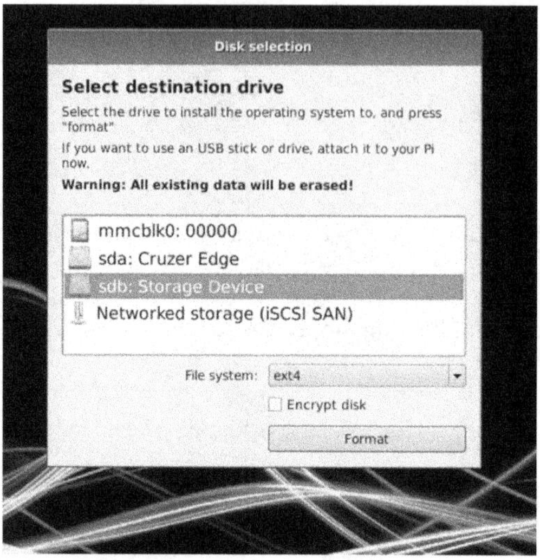

Figure 2-17. *Preparing to install BerryBoot to a drive*

Installing an OS with BerryBoot

After BerryBoot is installed, you can choose an operating system to download and install from the BerryBoot OS menu (Figure 2-18). Click **Popular** to choose from distros such as Raspbian, OpenElec, Android KitKat, Ubuntu with MATE desktop, and others. Click **Others** to choose from less-common distros including Raspbian Lite, Puppy Linux, Sugar, and others. Click **Appliances** to turn your Raspberry Pi into a specialized device.

Figure 2-18. *Details from BerryBoot's Popular, Others, and Appliances tabs*

To install a listed OS, click it and click **OK**. After the OS is downloaded and installed, click **OK** on the Installation Finished dialog to restart the system and boot the new OS.

To install a distro you downloaded manually:

1. Click **Cancel**.

2. After BerryBoot restarts, the BerryBoot menu editor appears.

3. Click and hold **Add OS**, and select **Copy OS from USB stick** (Figure 2-19).

Figure 2-19. *The BerryBoot menu editor preparing to install an OS from USB*

4. Navigate to a folder containing the OS you want to install.

5. Select it and click **Open** (Figure 2-20).

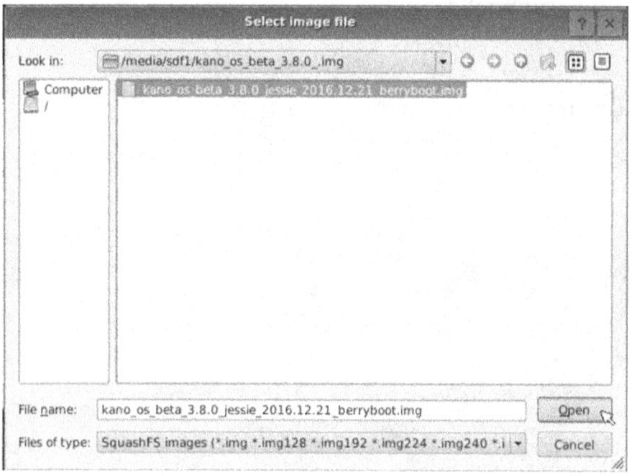

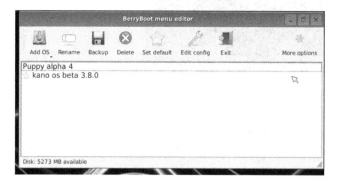

Figure 2-20. *Preparing to install Kano OS from a USB drive*

6. After BerryBoot copies the files, the OS is added to the boot menu.

To set up a multiboot configuration, open the **Add OS** menu and select an OS to download or install from USB. Figure 2-21 illustrates the menu editor after adding Puppy Linux via download and Kano OS from USB, setting Kano OS as the default OS, and renaming Kano OS from its original longer name.

Figure 2-21. *BerryBoot's multiboot, default OS, and renaming options in use*

To make a backup of an OS, select it and click **Backup**. You can back up the OS as originally configured, or with any changes you have made (installed packages, etc.). The **Edit config** options works the same way as in NOOBS or PINN, enabling you to edit startup files such as config.txt.

More Options for BerryBoot

Click **More options** to display the options shown in Figure 2-22. Select an OS and then click an option to use it:

- **Reset OS:** Sets the selected OS to its as-installed configuration.

- **Console:** Enables a BerryBoot console session. Press Ctrl-Alt-F2 to open the session (username: root, no password).

- **Set password:** Password-protects the selected OS.

- **Repair file system:** Runs fsck with the appropriate options.

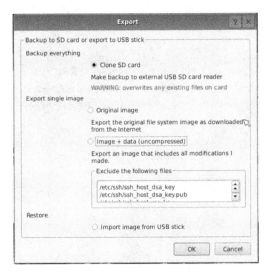

Figure 2-22. *BerryBoot's More Options menu*

- **Clone:** Opens the Export menu, which provides options for cloning the SD card, exporting an OS image, or importing an OS image (Figure 2-23).

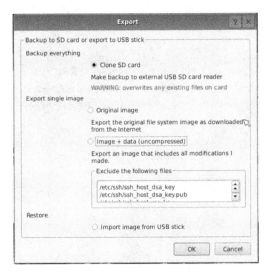

Figure 2-23. *BerryBoot's Export (Clone) menu*

Loading an OS with BerryBoot

The BerryBoot boot menu (Figure 2-24) appears after you restart your system or apply power to your system. If you selected a default OS, it boots unless you select another option (a different OS or the menu editor).

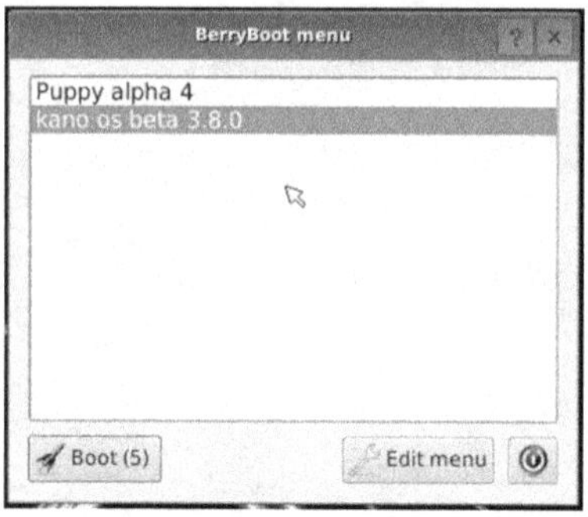

Figure 2-24. Preparing to load an OS from the BerryBoot boot menu

Other Linux Distros for Raspberry Pi

BerryBoot can install almost any Linux distro that is available in an appropriate image file format. Many of these can be downloaded from Alex Goldcheidt's BerryServer web site (http://berryboot.alexgoldcheidt.com/).

If you prefer to download a Linux distro directly from the creator's web site, here are some links for other popular and useful free distros:

FreeBSD

FreeBSD is based on BSD, a version of UNIX developed by the University of California, Berkeley. Available from www.freebsd.org/where.html (Links to R Pi-B and R Pi 2 SD card images). To get a version of FreeBSD for Raspberry Pi 3, go to http://www.raspbsd.org/raspberrypi.html. FreeBSD loads to the command line. Uname: freebsd PW: freebsd.

NetBSD

NetBSD is also based on BSD. Available from https://netbsd.org/releases/ (link to evbarm download).

Fedora and CentOS

Fedora is the basis for RedHat Enterprise. It is updated more frequently than RedHat and thus supports newer technologies more quickly than Fedora. Available from http://fedoraproject.org/wiki/Raspberry_Pi.

CentOS is a free version of RedHat Enterprise and is owned by RedHat. Like RedHat Enterprise, CentOS stresses stability and has less frequent updates than Fedora. Available from www.centos.org/, https://wiki.centos.org/Download (Links for R Pi 2, R Pi 3).

OpenWRT

OpenWRT, originally developed as an enhanced open source replacement for the firmware in many Ethernet and wireless Ethernet routers, can also be installed on the Raspberry Pi. Available from https://wiki.openwrt.org/toh/raspberry_pi_foundation/raspberry_pi.

Choosing the Best Distro for the Task

Start by determining what it is you want to do with your Raspberry Pi. If you want to use your Raspberry Pi as a computing appliance, you can choose from media playback distros, signage distros, router distros, and many others, some of which were described earlier in this chapter. To use your Raspberry Pi with Windows 10, choose the Windows 10 IoT.

For general-purpose computing, you have two options:

- Distros that are bundled with preinstalled apps and a GUI desktop

- Distros that include the command line only

Distros that include a lot of preinstalled apps and a GUI desktop such as Raspbian, Ubuntu MATE, or Kano OS get you started in a hurry. Kano OS (used by the Kano Computer Kit) is also an excellent choice for teaching elementary or middle school students how computers work.

Choose distros such as FreeBSD, Ubuntu Server, NetBSD, CentOS, or Fedora if you prefer to choose your own GUI, languages, and utilities.

Use an OS selector such as NOOBS or PINN or an OS selector and boot manager such as BerryBoot to make trying different distros easy.

Creating Your Media

If you have a microSD card with NOOBS already installed, you're ready to start. However, if you need an updated version, prefer to use PINN or BerryBoot, or want to download your preferred OS directly to a microSD card, you need to install some free utilities, especially if you use Windows or OSX as your preferred primary OS. Be sure to see the distro web site for specific media creation recommendations.

Windows

If you use Windows and want to create your own microSD (or SD) boot media for Raspberry Pi, you should download and install the following free apps:

- 7-Zip (www.7-zip.org/)

- SD Card Formatter (www.sdcard.org/downloads/formatter_4)

- FAT32 Format (www.ridgecrop.demon.co.uk/index.htm?guiformat.htm)

- Win32 Disk Imager (https://sourceforge.net/projects/win32diskimager/)

In most cases, you use the tools in the following order:

1. Use 7-Zip to uncompress image files for Raspberry Pi (it also works with other Linux and non-Linux distros as well as Windows ZIP files and other Windows archive files). 7-Zip can run from the context (right-click) menu in Windows Explorer or File Manager (Figure 2-25).

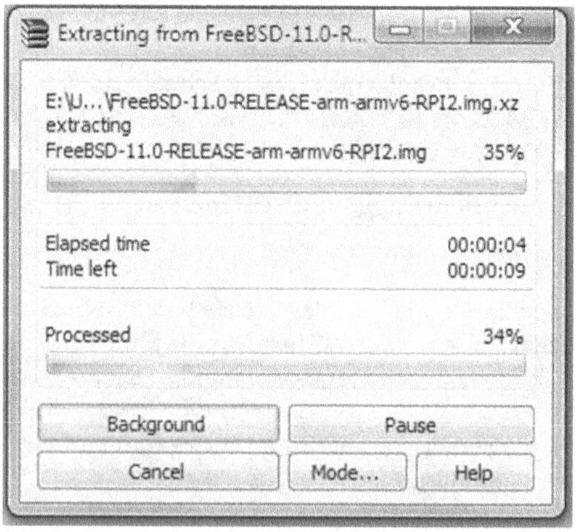

Figure 2-25. *Uncompressing a downloaded OS file using 7-Zip*

2. Use SD Card Formatter to format microSD or SD cards. It creates a FAT32 file system on cards, including cards previously formatted with other file systems. Turn on Format Size Adjustment to remove existing partitions (Figure 2-26).

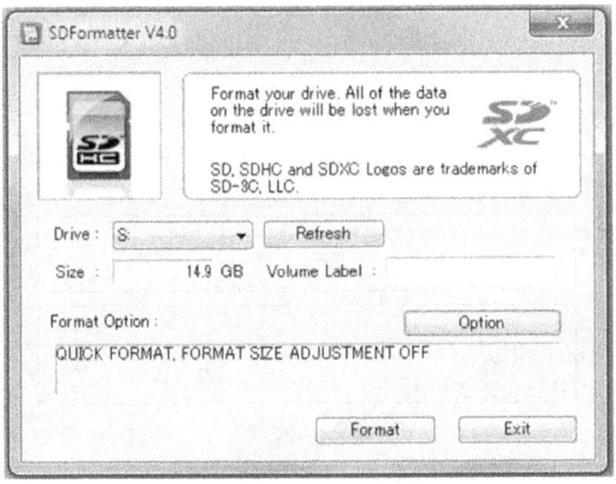

Figure 2-26. *Formatting a microSD card with SD Card Formatter*

3. If you want to use a 64GB SDXC card, you also need to format it with the FAT32 Format tool (guiformat.exe) so the drive is using the proper file system.

4. Use Win32 Disk Imager to write the image (.img) file that was uncompressed using 7-Zip to your media (Figure 2-27).

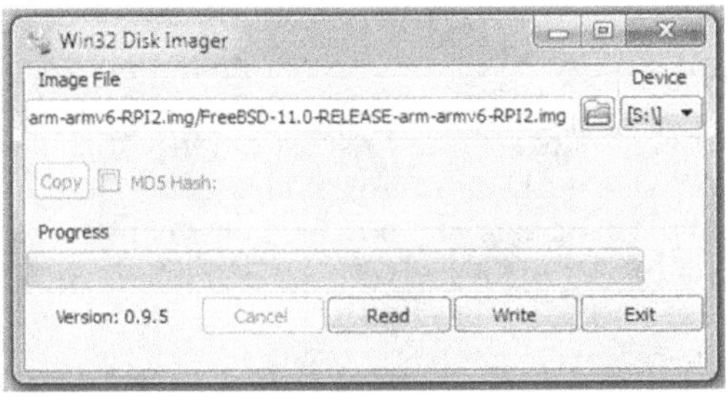

Figure 2-27. *Writing an OS image with Win32DiskImager*

■ **Note** Before using card format or disk imager apps, be sure to determine which drive letter is used by your microSD (SD, microSD in SD adapter) card. You don't want to format the wrong card (or your hard disk!) or write a 2GB image file over your 2TB hard disk's contents.

OSX (MacOS)

If you use OSX (MacOS) and want to create your own microSD (or SD) boot media for Raspberry Pi, you should download and install the following free apps:

- SD Card Formatter (www.sdcard.org/downloads/formatter_4)

- ApplePi-Baker (www.tweaking4all.com/hardware/raspberry-pi/macosx-apple-pi-baker/)

■ **Note** ApplePi-Baker should be used as a replacement for older OSX (macOS) GUI imaging apps recommended by most web sites. Versions of OSX (macOS) beginning with OSX 10.9 Mavericks do not work with older GUI imaging apps.

Linux

The Etcher utility available from http://etcher.io/ (also available for Windows and OSX/macOS) can be used to copy an image to a flash memory card. For other suggestions, see www.fossmint.com/3-best-gui-enabled-usb-image-writer-tools-on-linux/.

Summary

In addition to Raspian with PIXEL and Raspbian Lite, there are many operating systems designed for use with your Raspberry Pi. Choose the Linux distro or non-Linux OS to use based on whether you're wanting to run apps, create your own programs, or use your Pi as a retro gaming system, as a media player, or for specialized tasks. Utilities such as NOOBS, PENN, and BerryBoot make it easy to select the OS to install, and utilities available for Windows, MacOS, and Linux enable you to create customized installation media for your favorite operating systems.

CHAPTER 3

■ ■ ■

Adding Mass Storage

In this chapter, you will learn about using the Raspberry Pi's built-in MicroSD card slot, SD adapters for microSD cards, USB flash drives, USB card readers, and the WDLabs PiDrives made for Raspberry Pi. Depending upon the Raspberry Pi model in use, some USB drives might be connected via a USB 2.0 hub. Many of these devices are pictured in Figure 3-1.

Figure 3-1. *USB flash drive, card reader, microSD card, USB external hard disk, and WDLabs PiDrive*

Recommended Memory Card Types

Modern Raspberry Pi boards are designed to use microSD cards of at least 4GB in size if you are recording an image direct to the card (RISC OS, a non-Linux OS, can use a 2GB microSD card). For NOOBS and similar OS loaders and boot managers, at least 8GB is recommended.

© Mark Edward Soper 2017
M. E. Soper, *Expanding Your Raspberry Pi*, DOI 10.1007/978-1-4842-2922-4_3

The Raspberry Pi SD-cards page (`www.raspberrypi.org/documentation/installation/sd-cards.md`) recommends using at least a Class 6 card. While there are no official listings of tested cards, the following unofficial sources can be helpful when selecting cards to use.

- The eLinux RPi SD cards page `http://elinux.org/RPi_SD_cards`)

- The Raspberry Pi Dramble microSD cards Benchmarks (`www.pidramble.com/wiki/benchmarks/microsd-cards`)

The eLinux RPi card page has a user-supplied database of cards that are listed as working or not working along with details such as size, speed class, part number, notes, and date added.

The Dramble Benchmarks page shows over a dozen brand-name and generic cards tested on Raspberry Pi 2, Pi 3, and Pi 3 with overclocked card reader. Four tests were performed: hdparm buffered, dd write, 4K random read, 4K random write. The page also provides instructions on how to run speed tests yourself.

Tip To overclock the Raspberry Pi 3 card reader, use the following command to create a bash script (use 84 or 72 in place of 100 if you want to try this on a Raspberry Pi 2):

sudo bash -c 'printf "dtoverlay=sdhost,overclock_50=100\n" >> /boot/config.txt'

Reboot the computer and the card reader runs faster. For more details, see `www.jeffgeerling.com/blog/2016/how-overclock-microsd-card-reader-on-raspberry-pi-3`.

Figure 3-2 illustrates some of the microSD cards that can be used with a Raspberry Pi.

Figure 3-2. *8GB, 16GB, and 32GB microSD cards can be used by Raspberry Pi without reformatting. However, a 64GB card must be reformatted as FAT32 before it can be recognized.*

Table 3-1 provides a reference to microSD card speed ratings.

Table 3-1. *MicroSD Card Speed Ratings*

Card Speed	Write Speed*	Read Speed*	Notes
C4	4MBps		C-class cards do not have read-speed requirements
C6	6MBps		V6**
C8	8MBps		
C10	10MBps		V8
U1	10MBps	10MBps	V10
U3	30MBps	10MBps	V30

Sequential
**Video speed class ratings, card rating system for use in video recording.*
V90 (90MBps write) is the fastest.

▪ **Note** If you still use the original Model A or Model B Raspberry Pi boards that use full-size SD cards, you can also use microSD cards with a microSD to SD card adapter.

Expanding a Partition on a Flash Memory Card

Raspbian with PIXEL and many other Linux distros that include a desktop GUI use the full capacity of the memory card. However, some Linux distros and other operating systems made for the Raspberry Pi are configured to work with small-capacity (4GB or smaller) memory cards. To use the additional capacity of 8GB or larger cards, you must expand the partition after the OS is installed.

Table 3-2 lists some of the distros available for Raspberry Pi and whether their default installations use the entire capacity of a memory card by default.

Table 3-2. *Raspberry Pi Distros and Expanded Partitions*

Distro	Partition Exp.	Method
Raspian with PIXEL (also known as Raspian)	Yes	N/A
Raspbian Jesse Lite	Yes	N/A
CentOS	No	root-fs expand
RISC OS	No	SystemDisc app
FedBerry Minimal	No	fedberry-config
FedBerry	Yes	N/A

Determining the Current Partition Size (Parted)

There are a variety of utilities included in Linux distros that can be used for determining partition size. The most powerful one, because it can also be used to change partition sizes, is parted. However, it is easy to use parted to view partition sizes. Open a terminal session and run this command:

```
sudo parted -l
```

In Figure 3-3, parted is run from a terminal session in RaspEX to show that the entire 16GB capacity of the flash drive is in use.

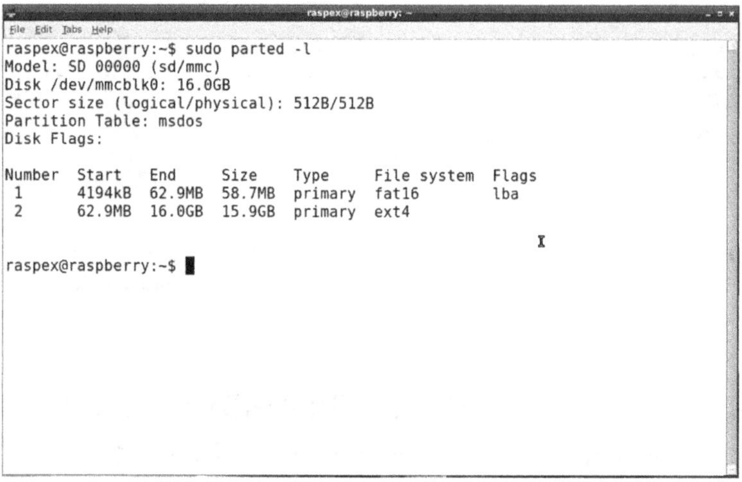

```
raspex@raspberry:~$ sudo parted -l
Model: SD 00000 (sd/mmc)
Disk /dev/mmcblk0: 16.0GB
Sector size (logical/physical): 512B/512B
Partition Table: msdos
Disk Flags:

Number  Start   End     Size    Type     File system  Flags
 1      4194kB  62.9MB  58.7MB  primary  fat16        lba
 2      62.9MB  16.0GB  15.9GB  primary  ext4

raspex@raspberry:~$
```

Figure 3-3. *RaspEx, which includes a GUI, uses the entire capacity of a 16GB memory card*

However, the CentOS distro shown in Figure 3-4 is using only 4GB of a 64GB microSD card (the card was formatted as FAT32 before CentOS was written to it).

```
[root@centos-rpi3 ~]# parted -l
Model: SD SL64G (sd/mmc)
Disk /dev/mmcblk0: 63.9GB
Sector size (logical/physical): 512B/512B
Partition Table: msdos
Disk Flags:

Number  Start   End     Size    Type     File system     Flags
 1      1049kB  525MB   524MB   primary  fat16           lba
 2      525MB   1062MB  537MB   primary  linux-swap(v1)
 3      1062MB  3210MB  2147MB  primary  ext4

[root@centos-rpi3 ~]#
```

Figure 3-4. *CentOS, which launches to the command line, is only using 3GB of the 64GB memory card it is installed on*

Expanding the Partition Using Parted

A disk partition that is not in use can be resized (expanded) by using the parted command-line tool. However, using parted requires that the system be booted up in rescue mode, which unmounts partitions and turns off swap space, or these changes must be made manually after a normal boot.

As an alternative, some Linux distros include resizing utilities that can be run without unmounting the current drive.

Expanding the Partition with RootFS-Expand (CentOS)

On current releases of CentOS, the Linux Root partition can be expanded to use the remaining space on the drive by using the root-fs expand utility. Rootfs-expand must be run using the root account:

```
/usr/local/bin/rootfs-expand
```

Tip   To switch to the root account, use the command **sudo su** (and provide the root user's password when prompted).

Figure 3-5 shows the output from rootfs-expand and parted -l to display the changed size of Partition 3.

```
Extending partition 3 to max size ....
CHANGED: partition=3 start=2074624 old: size=4194304 end=6268928 new: size=122660864,end=124735488
Resizing ext4 filesystem ...
resize2fs 1.42.9 (28-Dec-2013)
Filesystem at /dev/mmcblk0p3 is mounted on /; on-line resizing required
old_desc_blocks = 1, new_desc_blocks = 8
[ 1116.780262] EXT4-fs (mmcblk0p3): resizing filesystem from 524288 to 15332608 blocks
[ 1116.945104] EXT4-fs (mmcblk0p3): resized filesystem to 15332608
The filesystem on /dev/mmcblk0p3 is now 15332608 blocks long.

Done.
[root@centos-rpi3 ~]# parted
GNU Parted 3.1
Using /dev/mmcblk0
Welcome to GNU Parted! Type 'help' to view a list of commands.
(parted) quit
[root@centos-rpi3 ~]# parted -l
Model: SD SL64G (sd/mmc)
Disk /dev/mmcblk0: 63.9GB
Sector size (logical/physical): 512B/512B
Partition Table: msdos
Disk Flags:

Number  Start   End     Size    Type     File system     Flags
 1      1049kB  525MB   524MB   primary  fat16           lba
 2      525MB   1062MB  537MB   primary  linux-swap(v1)
 3      1062MB  63.9GB  62.8GB  primary  ext4

[root@centos-rpi3 ~]#
```

Figure 3-5. *Using rootfs-expand and parted -l to see the expanded partition on a system running CentOS*

Expanding the Partition Used by RISC OS

The version of RISC OS used by Raspberry Pi creates a RISC OS file system with a capacity of just under 2GB, even on larger flash drives. For this reason, preprogrammed RISC OS cards sold for use with Raspberry Pi are 2GB cards. To extend the RISC OS FileCore file system to use the entire capacity of larger microSD cards, use the SystemDisc utility available from Piccolo Systems (www.piccolosystems.com).

As an alternative, you might prefer to create an additional disk partition on the unused space. To learn how to create a FAT32 file system on a larger card, search the Raspberry Pi Forums at www.raspberrypi.org/forums for "RISCOS on a 4Gb SD Card" for instructions.

Connecting a USB Flash Drive or Memory Card

A flash memory card used with Linux needs to have at least one partition that uses a file system supported by the distro, typically ext4 or FAT32. Some distros, typically those with a GUI, automatically mount a flash memory card or USB card reader's card when it is connected. If not, follow this procedure (this example uses the Raspbian Jessie Lite distro):

1. Determine the currently connected drive and device name (Figure 3-6). To view the drive and device name (and partitions), use parted (see command syntax below Figure 3-6).

   sudo parted -l

```
pi@raspberrypi:~ $ sudo parted -l
Model: SD 00000 (sd/mmc)
Disk /dev/mmcblk0: 16.0GB
Sector size (logical/physical): 512B/512B
Partition Table: msdos
Disk Flags:

Number  Start    End      Size    Type     File system  Flags
1       4194kB   70.3MB   66.1MB  primary  fat32        lba
2       70.3MB   16.0GB   16.0GB  primary  ext4

pi@raspberrypi:~ $
```

Figure 3-6. *Using parted -l to display the disk name (mmcblk0) and partitions*

2. Create a folder that can be used as a mount point for the drive:

   sudo mkdir -p /media/USB

3. Connect the USB flash drive or insert a card into the card reader. If you are running a GUI, most systems will automatically display the name of the device when you connect it (and mount it for you). To list disks and partitions, use this command:

   sudo ls -1 /dev/disk/by-uuid

In this example (Figure 3-7), the new drive (listed first in this example) is known as **sda1** (device name is sda, partition #1). If a second drive is connected, it will be known as **sdb1**, and so on.

```
pi@raspberrypi:~ $ sudo ls -l /dev/disk/by-uuid
total 0
lrwxrwxrwx 1 root root 10 Mar  2 19:45 4FA0-1371 -> ../../sda1
lrwxrwxrwx 1 root root 15 Mar  2 19:33 adc806ed-d763-4eab-8319-b7ecfb276845 -> ../../mmcblk0p2
lrwxrwxrwx 1 root root 15 Mar  2 19:33 EF2C-AA8E -> ../../mmcblk0p1
pi@raspberrypi:~ $
```

Figure 3-7. *Using ls -l /dev/disk/by-uuid to display the device name and partition(s) on the newly connected drive*

4. Run **parted -l** again to see the file system used by the drive (in this example, shown in Figure 3-8, it is fat32). You need this information to mount the drive properly for use. Note that Linux refers to any USB storage device as Generic Mass-Storage (scsi).

```
pi@raspberrypi:~ $ sudo parted -l
Model: Generic Mass-Storage (scsi)
Disk /dev/sda: 15.9GB
Sector size (logical/physical): 512B/512B
Partition Table: msdos
Disk Flags:

Number  Start   End     Size    Type     File system  Flags
 1      4194kB  15.9GB  15.9GB  primary  fat32        lba


Model: SD 00000 (sd/mmc)
Disk /dev/mmcblk0: 16.0GB
Sector size (logical/physical): 512B/512B
Partition Table: msdos
Disk Flags:

Number  Start   End     Size    Type     File system  Flags
 1      4194kB  70.3MB  66.1MB  primary  fat32        lba
 2      70.3MB  16.0GB  16.0GB  primary  ext4


pi@raspberrypi:~ $ _
```

Figure 3-8. *Using parted -l to display the file system used by the new drive (fat32)*

5. Mount the drive as a read-only device into the folder created in Step 2 with

`sudo mount -t vfat /dev/sda1 /media/USB`

Note that vfat = FAT32. You can now use commands such as ls, cp (copies files from the device, and so on).

6. Unmount the drive with

`sudu umount /dev/sda1.`

Mounting a Drive for Read/Write Access

The preceding section covers how to mount a drive for read-only access from the command line. However, if you want to write to the drive (copy files to the drive, delete files on the drive, add a folder to the drive, or make other changes), you need to perform two additional tasks:

- Determine your uid and gid values
- Use that information as part of the syntax for a mount command

To determine your uid and gid, use the command **id**. These values are listed first. The values shown in Figure 3-9 may vary on systems with multiple users or if you are using the root account.

```
pi@raspberrypi:~ $ id
uid=1000(pi) gid=1000(pi) groups=1000(pi),4(adm),20(dialout),24(cdrom),27(sudo),29(audio),44(video),
  46(plugdev),60(games),100(users),101(input),108(netdev),997(gpio),998(i2c),999(spi)
pi@raspberrypi:~ $
```

Figure 3-9. *Using id to display uid and gid values for the current user*

Use this information in the mount syntax to use the drive as a read/write device:

```
mount -t vfat /dev/sda1 /media/USB -o rw,uid=1000,gid=1000,umask=133,dma
sk=022
```

You can delete files (rm) from the USB drive, copy files (cp) to the drive, make folders (mkdir) on the drive, and so on. The umount command is the same as before.

Partitioning a Flash Memory Card or USB Drive

Partitions on flash memory cards and USB drives prepared by Windows typically use the FAT32 file system. Although this file system is supported by Linux, the ext4 file system is a better choice if the partition will be used only by Linux or accessed over a network. Here's how to create an ext4 partition and file system. The following assumes that the existing partition contains no data (it will be removed in the process).

Caution The existing partition on the drive will be destroyed and recreated. Be sure to copy any data needed to another location before starting this process! If you must change partition types or sizes on a drive containing data without losing data, use Gparted (gparted.org).

1. Connect the drive.

2. Mount the drive as a read/write device.

3. Use fdisk to start the repartitioning process:

   ```
   sudo fdisk /dev/sda
   ```

4. Type m to see available commands (Figure 3-10).

```
pi@raspberrypi:~ $ ls /media/USB
PRR-1.jpg  PRR-2.jpg  PRR-3.jpg
pi@raspberrypi:~ $ sudo fdisk /dev/sda

Welcome to fdisk (util-linux 2.25.2).
Changes will remain in memory only, until you decide to write them.
Be careful before using the write command.


Command (m for help): m

Help:

  DOS (MBR)
   a   toggle a bootable flag
   b   edit nested BSD disklabel
   c   toggle the dos compatibility flag

  Generic
   d   delete a partition
   l   list known partition types
   n   add a new partition
   p   print the partition table
   t   change a partition type
   v   verify the partition table

  Misc
   m   print this menu
   u   change display/entry units
   x   extra functionality (experts only)

  Save & Exit
   w   write table to disk and exit
   q   quit without saving changes

  Create a new label
   g   create a new empty GPT partition table
   G   create a new empty SGI (IRIX) partition table
   o   create a new empty DOS partition table
   s   create a new empty Sun partition table


Command (m for help):
```

Figure 3-10. *Running fdisk on a mounted flash drive*

5. Type p to list the partitions on the selected drive.

6. Type d to delete the partition.

7. Type w to write changes to the partition and exit.

8. Restart fdisk as in Step 3.

9. Type p to view current partitions (no partitions should be visible [Figure 3-11]).

```
pi@raspberrypi:~ $ sudo fdisk /dev/sda

Welcome to fdisk (util-linux 2.25.2).
Changes will remain in memory only, until you decide to write them.
Be careful before using the write command.


Command (m for help): p
Disk /dev/sda: 14.9 GiB, 15931539456 bytes, 31116288 sectors
Units: sectors of 1 * 512 = 512 bytes
Sector size (logical/physical): 512 bytes / 512 bytes
I/O size (minimum/optimal): 512 bytes / 512 bytes
Disklabel type: dos
Disk identifier: 0x00000000
```

Figure 3-11. *Fdisk displays no partitions on the drive.*

10. Type n to create a new partition.

11. Type p to create a primary partition.

12. Type 1 to create the first primary partition.

13. Press Enter to use the default value for the first partition.

14. Press Enter to use the default value for the second partition.

15. Type w to write the new partition table and exit (Figure 3-12).

```
Command (m for help): n
Partition type
   p   primary (0 primary, 0 extended, 4 free)
   e   extended (container for logical partitions)
Select (default p): p
Partition number (1-4, default 1): 1
First sector (2048-31116287, default 2048):
Last sector, +sectors or +size{K,M,G,T,P} (2048-31116287, default 31116287):

Created a new partition 1 of type 'Linux' and of size 14.9 GiB.

Command (m for help): w
The partition table has been altered.
Calling ioctl() to re-read partition table.
Syncing disks.
```

Figure 3-12. *Creating a new partition with fdisk*

Formatting a Drive with ext4 File System

After a new partition has been created with fdisk, it must be formatted. Linux uses the **mkfs** utility to perform this task. If you don't specify the file system, mkfs defaults to the old ext2 file system. You must also specify the device. To create an ext4 file system on /dev/sda1, use the command shown in Figure 3-13:

sudo mkfs.ext4 /dev/sda1

```
pi@raspberrypi:~ $ sudo mkfs.ext4 /dev/sda1
mke2fs 1.42.12 (29-Aug-2014)
Creating filesystem with 3889280 4k blocks and 972944 inodes
Filesystem UUID: 8a983839-1869-4a01-b030-6be16340e032
Superblock backups stored on blocks:
        32768, 98304, 163840, 229376, 294912, 819200, 884736, 1605632, 2654208

Allocating group tables: done
Writing inode tables: done
Creating journal (32768 blocks): done
Writing superblocks and filesystem accounting information: done

pi@raspberrypi:~ $
```

Figure 3-13. *Using mkfs to create a file system on a drive partitioned with ext4*

Adding and Using an External Hard Drive

If more storage space is needed than is available on a USB flash drive or microSD memory card, you can use a USB hard drive with your Raspberry Pi. Using a USB hard drive, particularly a mechanical drive (non-SSD), is recommended if you are using your Raspberry Pi for logging, DVR media recording, or other apps that involve a lot of data writing and rewriting.

If your Linux distro has a GUI installed, the drive is mounted automatically. If you are using Linux without a GUI, you must mount the drive manually.

You can connect either a bus-powered or self-powered USB hard drive to a Raspberry Pi. We recommend using a USB 2.0 powered hub if you prefer to use bus-powered USB drives, especially with Raspberry Pi boards that use a 2A or smaller power supply.

Raspberry Pi boards have a limit of 1.2A total current draw for all USB ports, and default to providing a maximum of 600mA per port. Some bus-powered USB drives might not work properly with this limit. On B+, Pi 2, and Pi 3 boards, the following setting in the config.txt file can be used to raise the per-port amperage limit to 1.2A:

max_usb_current=1

■ **Note**   Config.txt is located in the /boot folder. You must be logged in as root (use **sudo su** to change to the root account).

To use a USB drive (hard disk or flash) as the root file system (in other words, to boot from the external drive), you must

1.   Determine which drive is the external drive.

2.   Clone the current boot drive to the external drive (the external drive's contents will be overwritten).

3.   Change boot parameters to use the external drive as root. The Raspberry Pi's onboard microSD/SD card is used to direct the system to boot from the external drive.

Note   The Adafruit web site has a complete step-by-step procedure and scripts to run to perform this process. Go to `https://learn.adafruit.com/external-drive-as-raspberry-pi-root/`.

Adding and Using a WDLabs Pi Drive

As noted in the previous section, Raspberry Pi boards can be connected to USB hard drives as well as USB flash drives or card readers. However, there are several issues to consider:

- Making effective use of the large storage space. For many users, a multiboot configuration is the best way to manage this space.

- Power requirements. A power supply that provides less than 2.0A may prevent a bus-powered USB drive from working. A marginal power supply may cause the Raspberry Pi to display a 20-pixel-square RGB rainbow box in the upper right-hand side of the display.

- Desktop clutter. A Raspberry Pi board uses very little desk space, but connecting it to a USB hard drive makes the combination about twice the size with plenty of cables everywhere.

Western Digital's line of WD Labs PiDrives are designed to help overcome each of these issues:

- The PiDrive Node Zero (314GB hard disk) and PiDrive Foundation Editions (250GB or 375GB hard disk) include a customized version of NOOBS that can load multiple instances of Raspbian Lite OS into as many as five partitions on the drive. These partitions are referred to as Project Spaces by Western Digital (Figure 3-14). Each instance of Raspbian Lite can be customized individually. At startup, you can choose which instance to boot.

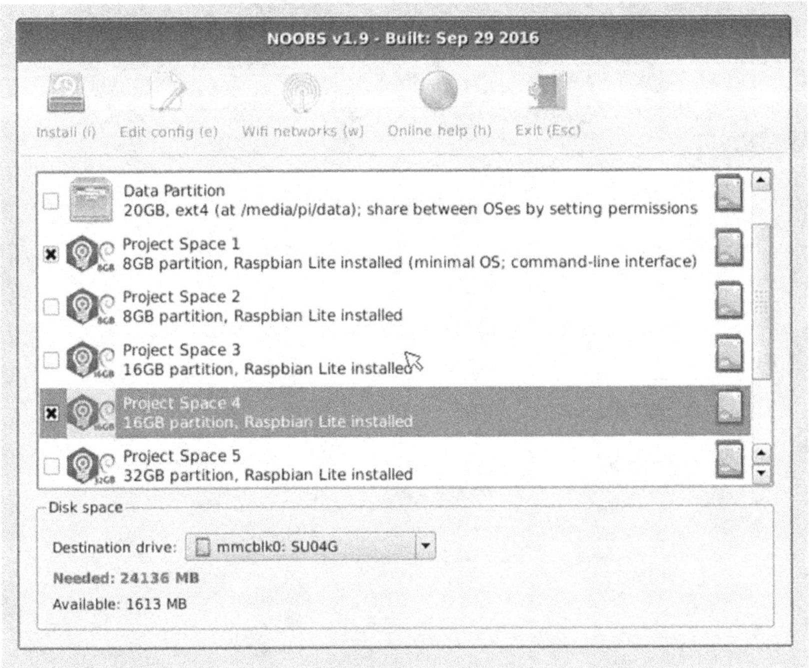

Figure 3-14. *PiDrive's version of NOOBS is preparing to install multiple copies of Raspbian Lite into separate Project Space partitions*

- The PiDrive BerryBoot Edition (1TB hard disk) includes a customized version of BerryBoot. BerryBoot can be used to install different operating systems onto the drive. Each OS can use the remaining free space on the drive, so it is not necessary to manually resize installed OS images (Figure 3-15).

Note You can download WD's PiDrive Foundation Edition Software (based on NOOBS) or BerryBoot from `http://wdlabs.wd.com/downloads/`.

Figure 3-15. *Sugar, a child-oriented version of Linux available through BerryBoot, can access all of the remaining disk space on the WDLabs PiDrive*

- To reduce desktop and cable clutter, the PiDrive Foundation Edition and BerryBoot editions include a PiDrive cable that can power the hard drive and Raspberry Pi from a single power source (Figure 3-16).

Figure 3-16. *WDLabs offers a 3A (shown) power supply and USB cable that provides plenty of power to run both a PiDrive and a full-size or smaller Raspberry Pi board through the special PiDrive cable*

WDLabs Pi Drives are also customized to use less power than standard 2.5-in. hard disks and can be installed along with the Raspberry Pi in cases that provide easy access to the Raspberry Pi's board connectors.

The PiDrive Node Zero features a specially designed daughterboard that enables a Raspberry Pi Zero, which normally has one Micro-USB port, to feature two full-size USB ports and use only one cable to power both board and drive. In Figure 3-17, the daughterboard, drive, and Pi Zero board are shown without the mounting hardware that holds them together.

Note   Western Digital has stopped producing PiDrive hardware products. However, these products will be sold as long as inventory is available. See http://wdlabs.wd.com/ category/wd-pidrive/ for details.

Figure 3-17. *WDLabs PiDrive Node Zero uses this daughterboard (shown without mounting hardware) to connect to the Pi Zero's Micro-USB data and power ports and the PiDrive's USB port*

Wireless Drives

Wireless drives are available in both hard disk and USB flash memory form factors. Because they connect to the Raspberry Pi via Wi-Fi, they will be discussed in Chapter 4.

Troubleshooting

Typical problems with mass storage on Raspberry Pi include the following:

- Incorrectly formatted media

- Not enough power

- Drive can't be mounted in read/write mode

- Defective cables

Incorrectly Formatted Media

If a flash memory card is not properly formatted (FAT32, ext4, or other file systems supported by Linux), it cannot be recognized by the Raspberry Pi board and the system will not start it. 64GB or larger microSD cards must be formatted as FAT32 before they can be used on a Raspberry Pi.

Reformat the card and be sure to use an OS supported by the Raspberry Pi board (see Chapter 2 for details).

If a boot manager (NOOBS, BerryBoot, PINN, and so on) cannot locate the OS after installation, make sure the drive where the OS is located is working. If the OS is on a USB drive, make sure the drive is plugged in and powered on. If the drive is connected to a USB port via a cable, make sure the cable is designed to support USB 2.0 or faster speeds (very thin cables are not recommended). With BerryBoot, open the Options menu and use the Repair File System option if the drive is properly inserted or connected but is not working.

Not Enough Power

If you are using a USB hard drive with have at least a 2A power supply and are not using all of the USB ports on the Pi, use the config.txt option to increase maximum USB port power. With a Pi Zero, upgrade to a higher-amperage power supply as the typical bundled power supply is only 1A.

With a Pi B+, Pi 2, or Pi 3, consider using a 3A power supply if you use bus-powered USB drives, The WDLabs PiDrive cable can be purchased separately (see https://www.wdc.com/products/wdlabs/wd-pidrive-cable.html or third-party vendors) to simplify cable management, and it works with any bus-powered USB drive that uses the standard USB 3.0 micro-B connector.

With any Pi model, consider using a powered USB 2.0 hub to enable multiple devices (including drives) to be connected to a separate power supply from the Pi.

Caution   Some 2.5-inch enclosures used to convert internal SATA laptop drives into external drives use a USB 3.0 Type A cable for the drive connection.

Drive Can't Be Mounted in Read/Write Mode

One of the advantages of working with external storage devices with a Linux GUI is that drives are normally mounted automatically in read/write mode when you connect them. However, Linux checks drives for possible errors (so-called "dirty drives") and will mount them in read-only mode if the drive might have errors (due to incorrect ejection from a host computer, etc.). If you are unable to write to a USB drive that was mounted in read/write mode, use the command dmesg to view drive-related events:

sudo dmesg

Summary

To get the most out of your Raspberry Pi, make sure you understand how to expand the storage space used by your preferred operating system to use the full capacity of your flash memory. Learn commands for mounting a new drive and using it in read/write mode if you use a command-prompt (non-GUI) Linux distro or other operating system. If you want to have a multiboot configuration so you can choose the operating system to run when you start your Pi, consider adding a USB hard disk to store and access your operating systems.

## CHAPTER 4

Connecting to a Workgroup Network

In this chapter, you will learn how to connect your Raspberry Pi to workgroup networks found in home office and small business environments using wired or wireless connections. Your Raspberry Pi will need a working wireless network connection, using either integrated wireless hardware (Raspberry Pi 3 or the Raspberry Pi Zero W) or an RPi-compatible Wi-Fi USB adapter. Most topics also support a wired Ethernet adapter.

Distro and Raspberry Pi Configuration

To connect to workgroup networks, Linux uses Samba. Samba is an open source implementation of Windows SMB networking. Many distros already have Samba installed, so if you only want to connect to shared folders, your Raspberry Pi may already be ready to connect. However, unless you already have a user ID on systems with shared resources, you will need to set up a user account on those systems. The following example assumes that a user called pi has been added to the user accounts on the Windows or OSX (MacOS) share.

Connecting to a Windows Share with PIXEL

To connect to a Windows share from Raspbian with PIXEL, follow this procedure:

1. Open the distro's file manager.

2. Enter **smb://servername/sharename**. (Replace servername/
   sharename with actual server name and share name: see
   Figure 4-1.) If you prefer, you can also enter **smb://WORKGROUP**
   (use the actual name of your workgroup) to see a list of servers
   with PIXEL or FedBerry. You can then navigate to the server
   needed.

© Mark Edward Soper 2017
M. E. Soper, *Expanding Your Raspberry Pi*, DOI 10.1007/978-1-4842-2922-4_4

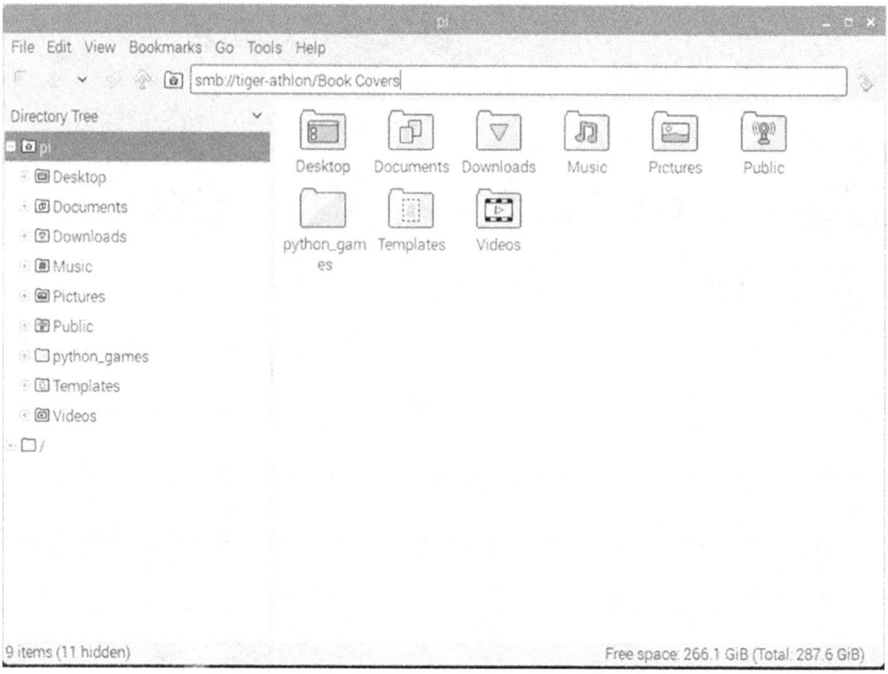

Figure 4-1. Entering the path to a shared folder on a server on the local network

3. When prompted, provide the username and password for the sharename (Figure 4-2).

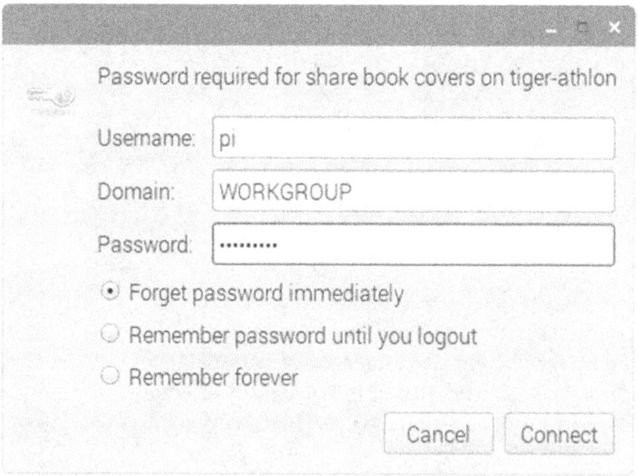

Figure 4-2. Logging into the server

4. Select how long to retain the password, then click Connect.

5. The share opens (Figure 4-3).

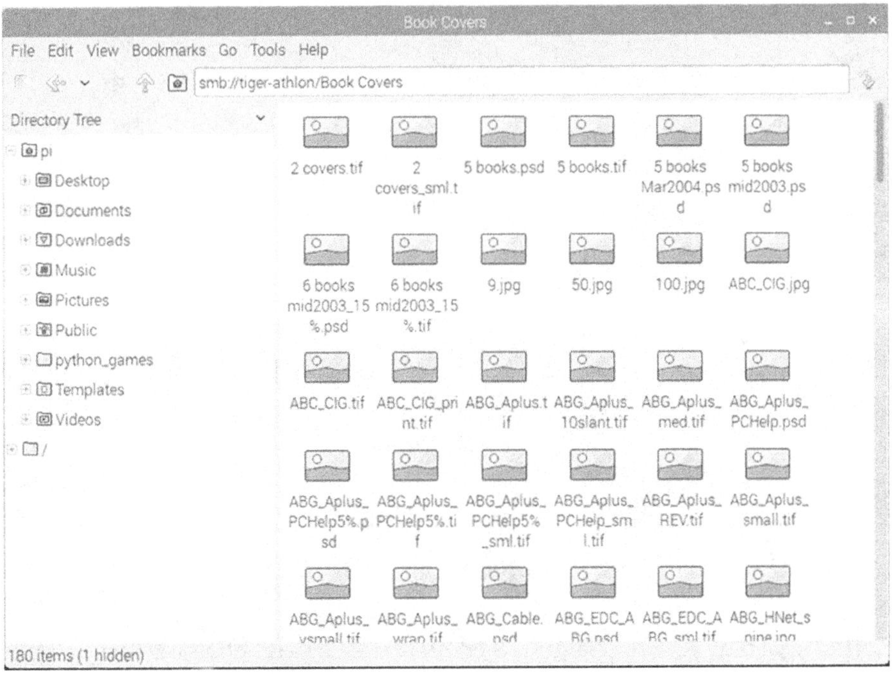

Figure 4-3. *Contents of the share as viewed in PIXEL*

Some other file managers, such as the one in Ubuntu MATE (Figure 4-4), can display network shares without the need to enter a path.

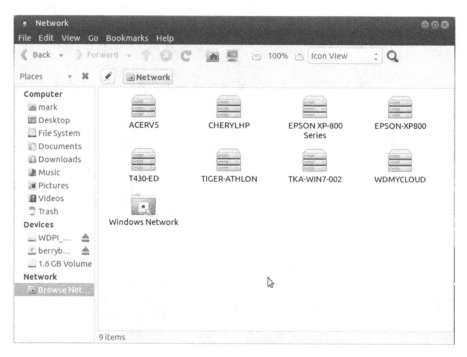

Figure 4-4. *Navigating to a Windows share with Ubuntu MATE*

Connecting to a Windows Share from the Command Line with smbclient

To connect to a Windows share from the command line, use **smbclient**. This might not be preinstalled on minimal distros for Raspberry Pi, but it can be installed from your distro's package manager.

■ **Tip**　To assure that you are getting the latest version of packages, run `sudo apt-get update` before installing any packages. When installing any package, some package components might not be available on the first try. Rerun the install command to load any packages that did not install on the first attempt.

To determine if smbclient is already installed, run it from the command line. If you get a **command not found error**, you will need to install smbclient. From a terminal prompt, run **sudo apt-get install smbclient**. To connect with a remote server and download a file:

1. Enter **smbclient//servername/sharename**.

2. When prompted, enter the password for the username.

3. When the **smb: \>?** prompt appears, you are logged into the remote computer. You can use commands to list files (**ls**) and other file management commands.

4. To copy a file from the remote computer: enter **get filename.ext**.

5. To close the connection, enter quit.

▓ **Note** If the sharename is more than one word, for example, Jim's Files, surround it with double-quotes: `smbclient//servername/"share name"`.

Connecting to Different Workgroups

During the login process, you can specify the name of the workgroup you are connecting with. If you are using a file manager, the login window prompts you for the workgroup or domain name (refer to Figure 4-2). You can replace the default WORKGROUP name with the name of the workgroup you are connecting with. Some file managers may use Samba as the default domain. With the command line smbclient, the -W=workgroup option is used to set the workgroup if it is different from the default name WORKGROUP. When connecting to a Windows share, it may not be necessary to specify the workgroup. Try the connection without specifying the workgroup name.

The situation is much different if you want to configure your Raspberry Pi to receive connections from other computers. You must install Samba's server features. And, if the workgroup is not named WORKGROUP, you must also create (or modify) the /etc/smb. conf file to indicate the correct workgroup name.

Connecting to an OSX (MacOS) Share from Raspbian PIXEL

The process of connecting to an OSX (MacOS) share from Raspbian Pixel is similar to the process for connecting to a Windows share, but with one major difference: use Apple File Protocol (afp://) instead of smb://.:

1. Open the distro's file manager.

2. Enter **afp://servername**.

3. When prompted, provide the username and password for the sharename (Figure 4-5).

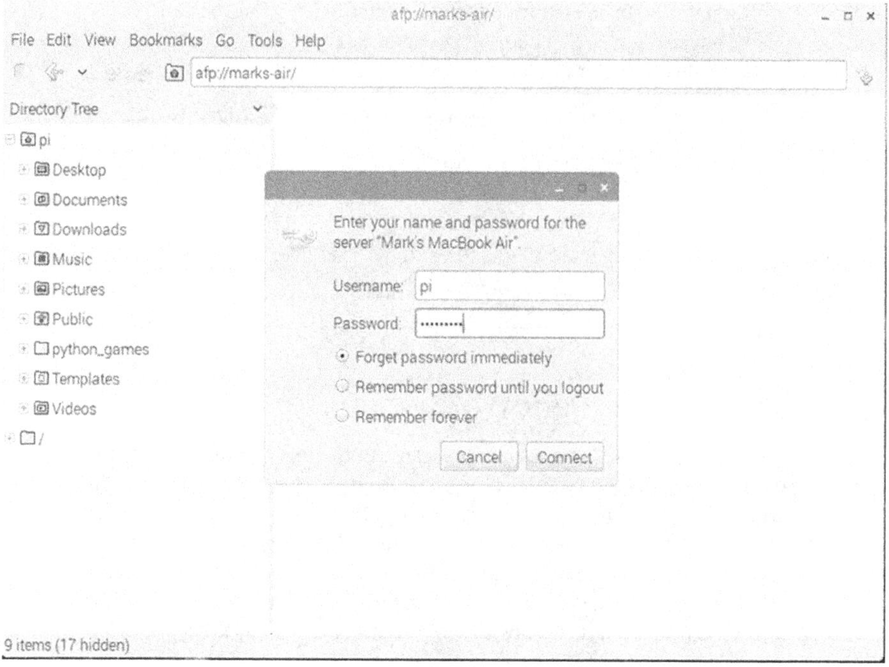

Figure 4-5. *Logging into a MacOS (OSX) share with Raspbian with PIXEL*

4. Select how long to retain the password, then click Connect.

5. Select a share.

6. Log in again if prompted, using the same username and password as in Step 3.

7. The share opens (Figure 4-6).

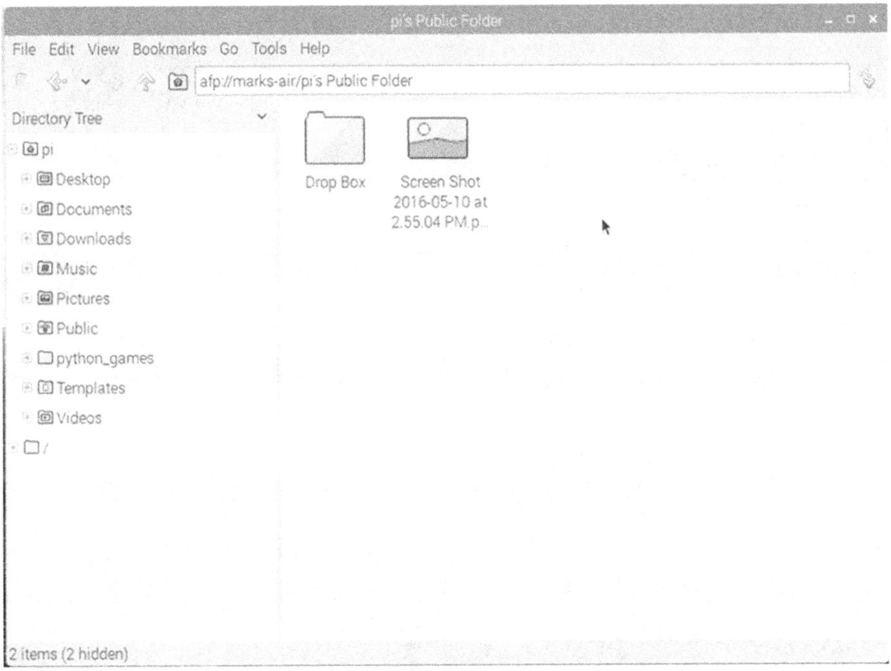

Figure 4-6. Working with a MacOS (OSX) share with Raspbian with PIXEL

■ **Note** To configure an OSX share and determine the correct address, open **Settings ➤ Sharing ➤** turn on **File Sharing**, and note the correct afp:// path to the share. Select the folder to share, the user(s) to share it with, and the share level (read or read/write). Create a new user at **Settings ➤ Users and Groups**.

Using Wireless Drives

Wireless drives are available in both hard disk and USB flash memory form factors from vendors such as Seagate, Western Digital, SanDisk, and others. In this section, we discuss using SanDisk and Seagate wireless drives. To connect to a wireless drive from a Raspberry Pi, you must know the following:

- The device's IP address
- The device's home folder
- The login username (and password, if required)

Connecting to a SanDisk Connect Wireless Flash Drive

The SanDisk Connect wireless flash drive supports WebDAV for read access, so you can access its contents via your Raspberry Pi's web browser. To configure the device to be available on an existing wireless network:

1. Install the SanDisk Connect app on an iOS or Android smartphone or tablet.

2. Start the app and connect to the SanDisk wireless flash drive.

3. Open the **Settings** menu.

4. Turn on **Internet connection**.

5. Connect to the wireless network you normally use. Provide the encryption key for the network if prompted.

For details, see https://kb.sandisk.com/app/answers/detail/a_id/3802/.

■ **Note**   The SanDisk Connect wireless flash drive is primarily designed to work as a wireless media source for Android and iOS mobile devices.

To determine the IP address for the wireless flash drive:

1. Start the app and connect to the SanDisk wireless flash drive.

2. Open the **Settings** menu.

3. Tap **About**.

4. Tap **WFD** in the Drives listing.

5. Note the drive's IP address.

To connect to the wireless flash drive:

1. Start your Raspberry Pi and open the web browser.

2. Enter the IP address and file location: http://192.168.x.x/wfd/ (use the actual IP address values in place of the example values). See Figure 4-7.

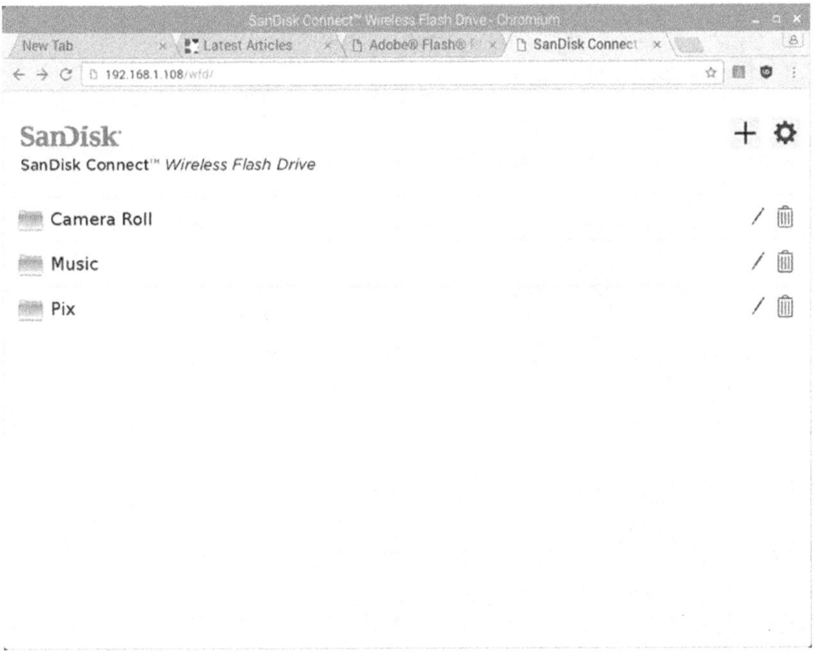

Figure 4-7. Connecting to a SanDisk Connect wireless flash drive using the Chromium browser

3. The folders on the drive are visible. Open a folder to view, open, or download drive contents.

Note Unfortunately, you cannot make any changes to the files or folders on the SanDisk drive when you connect wirelessly. To write to the drive or make other changes, connect it to a USB port on your Raspberry Pi or other computer. It behaves just like any other flash drive when connected via USB.

Connecting to a Seagate Wireless Plus Drive

The Seagate Wireless Plus drive is primarily designed to work as a wireless media source for Android and iOS mobile devices. However, it also supports uploading as well as downloading through its web interface. You can connect to the drive wirelessly and also access your normal wireless network. Here's how.

1. Turn on the Seagate Wireless Plus drive.

2. The green light is the power light; the blue light is the Wi-Fi light.

3. When the Wi-Fi light remains on (stops blinking), open the Wi-Fi connection dialog on your Raspberry Pi and click the Seagate Wireless FMP icon (Figure 4-8).

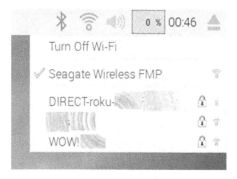

Figure 4-8. *Connecting to a Seagate Wireless Plus drive using Raspbian with PIXEL's wireless connection manager*

4. After verifying your connection, open your web browser and navigate to http://172.25.0.1.

5. The Seagate Wireless Plus drive opens. To reconnect to the Internet, click the Wi-Fi icon (Figure 4-9).

Figure 4-9. *Preparing to connect to the default wireless network through the Seagate Wireless Plus's network dialog*

6. Choose your wireless network.

7. Enter the encryption key (wireless password). If you plan to use this drive frequently, click the "Connect to this network automatically" box. If you are using the drive on a public network, click the "Secure the network" box.

8. Click "Join network."

9. Click OK. When the screen refreshes, you are connected to the drive and to your normal wireless network.

You can view, play back, or download content from the Seagate Wireless Plus, but, unlike the SanDisk Wireless drive, you can also upload content to the drive from the Raspberry Pi:

1. Click the upload icon (refer to Figure 4-9).

2. Click **Browse**.

3. Navigate to the location of the file you want to upload.

4. Click the file, then click **Open**.

5. Click **Upload**. The dialog box confirms that the file is uploaded.

░ **Note** You can download multiple files from the drive by checking them. However, if you want to copy multiple files to the drive, connect it to a USB port on your Raspberry Pi or other computer. It behaves just like any other hard drive when connected via USB.

As long as you are connected wirelessly to the Seagate Wireless Plus, it will pass Internet traffic to and from your wireless network. When the drive is turned off, you must reconnect manually to your normal wireless network. The drive can be configured through its web interface (change the default SSID, require passwords for connection, and so on).

Printing to a Network Printer

To print from a Raspberry Pi to a USB or network printer, you must install CUPS (Common Unix Printing System). To install CUPS, open a terminal session and use the following command:

```
sudo apt-get install cups
```

Configuring CUPS

After installing CUPS, you need to add your user account (pi) to the default user group created by CUPS (lpadmin):

```
sudo usermod -a -G lpadmin pi
```

CUPS is configured through your web browser. By default, you must use the web browser on your Raspberry Pi, using the loopback interface. 631 is the post number used by CUPS. Either of the following addresses in your web browser will start CUPS:

```
http://127.0.0.1:631
http://localhost:631
```

■ **Tip**   To configure CUPS to be configured from any computer on your network, you can modify the cupsd.conf file. For details, see www.howtogeek.com/169679/how-to-add-a-printer-to-your-raspberry-pi-or-other-linux-computer/.

The CUPS opening dialog (Figure 4-10) has options for users, administrators, and developers. To add a printer, open the Administration tab. Follow these steps to add a printer:

1. Click **Add Printer**.

2. Log in with username and password to continue.

3. Select the printer. Note that physical printers, network printers, and print protocols are all available. In this example, I selected the Epson XP-800 series printer (Figure 4-10).

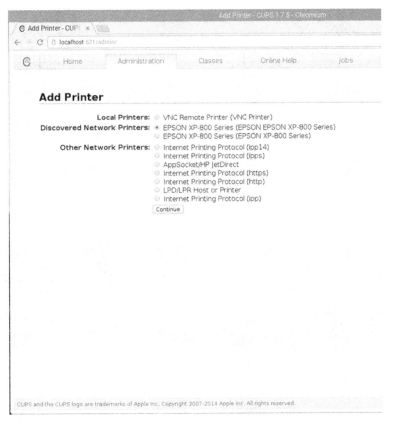

Figure 4-10. *Selecting a network printer with CUPS*

4. Confirm or change the name, description, and location
    (optional).

5. Click the box to share the printer with others (use only with a
    locally connected printer).

6. Click **Continue**.

7. Select your printer driver (Figure 4-11).

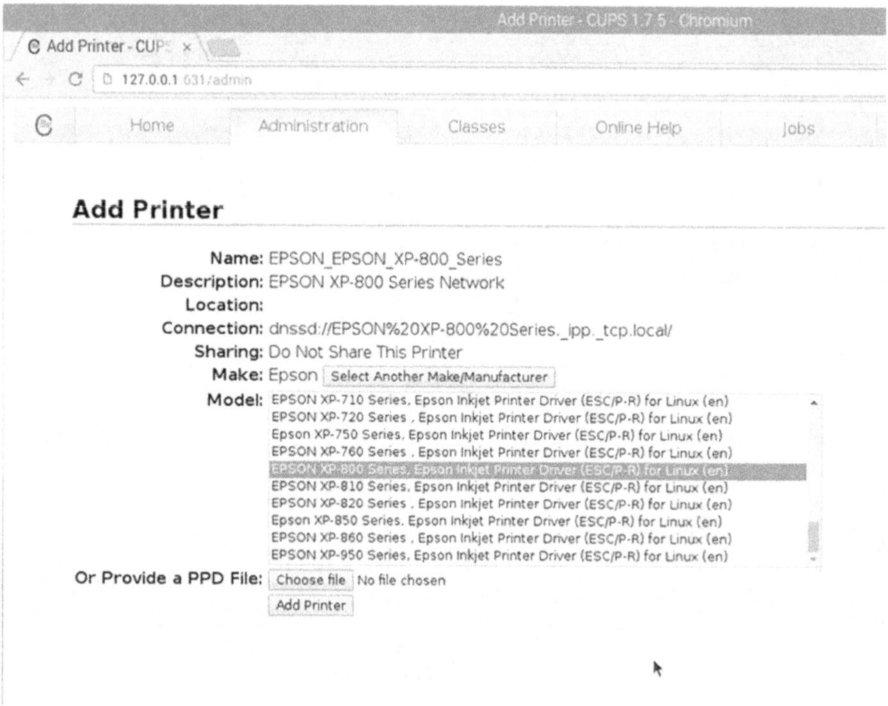

Figure 4-11. *Selecting a printer driver with CUPS*

8. Click **Add Printer**. The Set Default Options dialog (next section) opens.

■ **Note** If CUPS does not list your printer, exit CUPS. Search the software repositories for a driver for your printer and install it. Rerun CUPS after installing the updated driver and select it. If you are using a multifunction (print/scan device), you will use CUPS for printing and SANE for scanning.

Setting Printer Defaults

The Set Default Options for your printer are displayed next. Select the default paper size, paper or media type, and other settings you will most typically use. When you are finished selecting options, click **Set Default Options**.

Testing Your Printer

To determine if you can connect to the printer, open the Maintenance menu and select **Print Self Test Page**. The printer will print a self-test page, such as a printhead color pattern or other default (varies with printer). To test fonts, colors, and graphics settings, create a document and print it.

■ **Note**   To learn how to set up your Raspberry Pi to act as a print and scan server, see Chapter 6.

Scanning with a Network Scanner

To scan to a local or network scanner (including multifunction devices), use SANE (Scanner Access Now Easy). To learn more about SANE, go to www.sane-project.org/. SANE is an application programming interface (API) for scanning. SANE calls the graphical and command-line apps that use SANE for scanning as frontends. The drivers used by SANE to connect to a particular scanner are known as backends. In other words, to scan to a local or network scanner, download SANE, one or more frontends, and the backend (driver) needed for your scanner. Keep in mind that some scanners and multifunction devices are not compatible with SANE. Check the SANE database of compatible devices and with your scanner or multifunction device vendor to determine compatibility.

■ **Note**   The process of installing SANE and its frontends and backends is identical for both network and USB connected scanners. For details, see Chapter 7.

Raspberry Pi Linux Samba Server Configuration

Raspbian with PIXEL is already ready to connect to Windows or MacOS (OSX) shares. However, if you want to share folders on Raspbian or other Linux distros on your Raspberry Pi, you must install Samba's server features. Open a terminal session to install these features:

```
sudo apt-get update
sudo apt-get install samba samba-common-bin
```

■ **Note**   You can install more than one package at a time by placing them on the command line as in this example. The first package in this example is samba, and the second is samba-common-bin, which adds support for commands such as testparm.

Creating Local Users

If you want to create additional users that can connect to a network share on your Raspberry Pi, you must first of all create them as local users. In the following example, replace **username** with the username you want to use, such as marcus:

1. **sudo adduser username**.

2. At the prompt **Enter new UNIX password:**, type the password you want to use.

3. At the prompt **Retype new UNIX password:**, retype the same password.

4. When prompted, you can enter user information (Full Name, Room Number, Work Phone, Home Phone, Other) or just press the Enter key.

5. Press Y if the information is correct. The new user is created (see Figure 4-12).

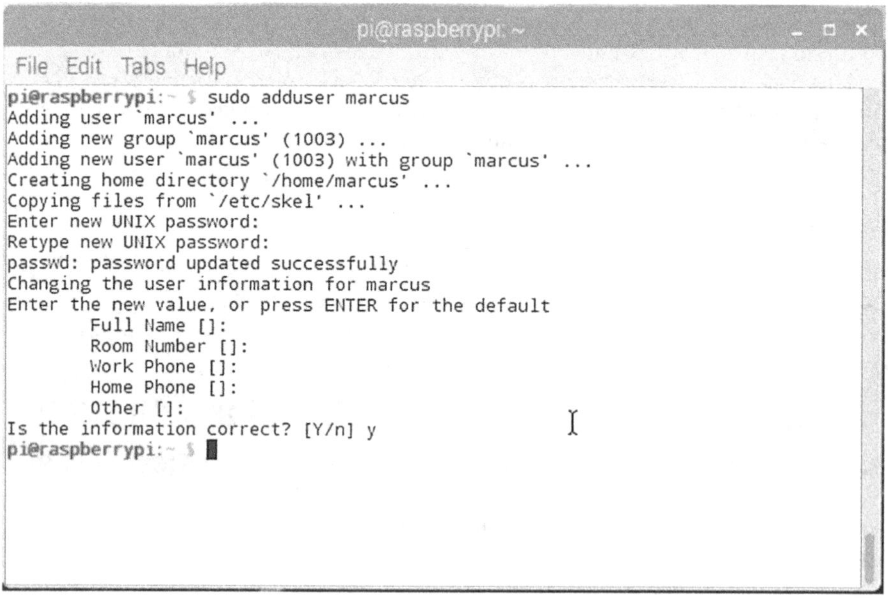

Figure 4-12. Setting up a new local user

Creating a Network User

To make the user pi a network user:

1. **sudo smbpasswd -a pi**

2. At the prompt **New smb password:**, type a password

3. At the prompt **Retype new smb password:.**, retype the same password

Repeat for any users you created in the **Creating Local Users** section.

Tip You can use separate UNIX (local access) and smb (network access) passwords for each user, but it's a lot easier to use the same password text for the UNIX and smb passwords for a given user. For example, if user marcus has the UNIX password **thisbook**, use **thisbook** for the smb password for marcus.

Configuring smb.conf

After installing Samba and setting up users, we need to determine which folder we want to share. Only the files and folders in the folder we share will be available to others on the network. You can create a new folder or use an existing folder, such as the user's home folder.

Samba has many configuration options. Some, but not nearly all, are stored as comments in the Samba configuration file /etc/samba/smb.conf. We need to configure the following:

- Workgroup name

- WINS support

- Folder to share

- How folder will be shared

To edit /etc/samba/smb.conf, open a terminal session and run this command:

```
sudo texteditor /etc/samba/smb.conf
```

(replace *texteditor* with leafpad, nano, or your preferred text editor)

The following statements need to be uncommented or added to smb.conf. To uncomment a statement, remove the ; from the front of the statement:

```
workgroup = WORKGROUP
wins support = yes
```

77

> ■ **Note**   Change the workgroup name WORKGROUP to the actual workgroup name.

If you created a folder called **share**, add the following section into the ===Share Definitions=== section to complete the needed configuration:

```
[pihome]
 comment = Pihome
 path = /home/pi/share
 nrowseable = Yes
 writeable = Yes
 only guest = no
 create mask = 0777
 directory mask = 0777
 public = no
```

Here's what each statement means:

- [pihome] - The following statements set up a shared folder on your Raspberry Pi

- comment = Pihome

- path = /home/pi/share - The folder being shared (**share**) is located beneath the pi folder; change **share** to the actual name of the folder

- browseable = Yes - The folder specified with path= can be viewed

- writeable = Yes - The folder specified with path= can be written (files saved, deleted, or changed by a network user) to as well as read (omit this for a read-only share)

- only guest = no - Disables guest access

- create mask = 0777 - Enables read/write/execute permission to all users who can log into the share; change to 0700 to make the share read-only

- directory mask = 0777 - Enables read/write/execute permission to all users who can log into the share; change to 0700 to make the share read-only

- public = no - Disables public access

> ■ **Note**   For more about mask values in Samba, see `https://lists.samba.org/archive/samba/2003-March/063429.html`. For a complete and well-cross-referenced guide to Samba configuration statements, see `www.samba.org/samba/docs/man/manpages/smb.conf.5.html`.

To enable each user to connect to its home folders with read/write access, make the following changes to the [Homes] section:

```
[Homes]
 Comment = Home Directories
 Browseable = no
 read-only = no
 writeable=Yes
 create mask=0775
 directory mask=0775
 valid users = %S
 username map = /etc/samba/sambausers
```

After completing these edits, save your changes. As a result of these changes, any smb (network) user will see two shares when they connect to the Raspberry Pi: the share folder and their personal folder (refer to Figure 4-15).

Logging into the Raspberry Pi

Here's how to log into your new Raspberry Pi share from a remote computer on the LAN:

1. Open your system's file manager.

2. Open Network.

3. Open RASPBERRYPI.

4. Enter your username and password when prompted and click OK (Figure 4-13).

Figure 4-13. Logging into a Raspberry Pi using Windows

5. Open your share (Figure 4-14).

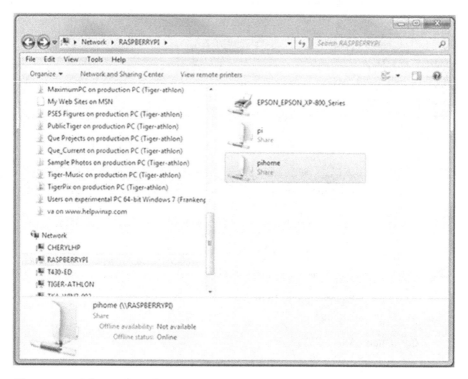

Figure 4-14. *Selecting from the remote user's home folder or the common share folder using Windows*

Connecting to Raspberry Pi from an Android Device

To connect to a Raspberry Pi share from Android, you can use one of these methods:

- Install a file management app on your mobile device and use it to connect to your Raspberry Pi share(s).

- Configure Raspberry Pi for SSH connections, configure your mobile device for SSH connections, and use FTP.

- Configure Raspberry Pi for SSH connections and install an SSH app on your mobile device. Some available apps include Connectbot (Android), JuiceSSH (Android), and Termius (Android, iOS, Windows, Linux, and MacOS).

If all you want is access to a shared file or folder on the Raspberry Pi, the first option is simpler.

⬚ **Note** Using SSH for headless booting and control of a Raspberry Pi is covered in Chapter 6.

The following example uses the free ES File Explorer, one of many file managers available from the Google Play store:

1. After installing ES File Explorer, open it on your Android device.

2. Open **menu** (three-bar icon) ➤ **Network** ➤ **LAN.**

3. Click **Scan** to detect all devices on the network.

4. Press and hold the RASPBERRYPI icon to check it.

5. Click **Edit Server.**

6. Turn off **Anonymous.**

7. Enter the username and password for your shared folder.

8. Click **OK** (Figure 4-15).

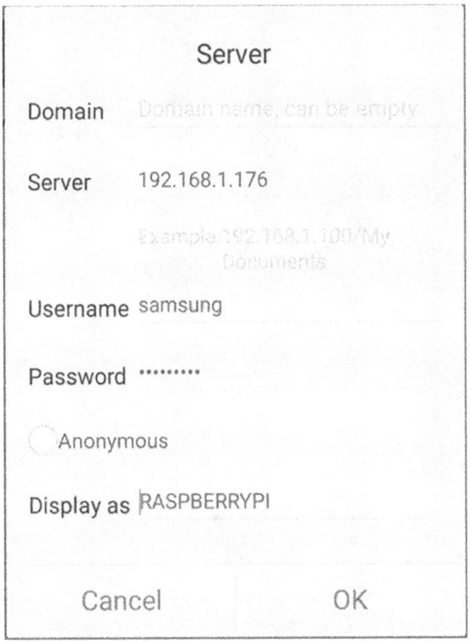

```
                    Server

Domain      Domain name, can be empty


Server      192.168.1.176

            Example: 192.168.1.100/My
                     Documents

Username    samsung


Password    •••••••••

  Anonymous

Display as   RASPBERRYPI


      Cancel              OK
```

Figure 4-15. *Configuring login information for the Raspberry Pi shares*

9. Navigate to the shared folder.

Connecting to Raspberry Pi from an iOS Device

As with Android, you can use a file management app or SSH to connect to a Raspberry Pi share from iOS. The following example uses the free File Explorer by Skyjos, one of many file managers available from the app store:

1. After installing File Explorer, open it on your iOS device.

2. Click the plus (+) sign to set up a new connection.

3. Click Linux/Unix from the New Connection list.

4. Scroll down and select RASPBERRYPI from Network Neighborhood (Figure 4-16).

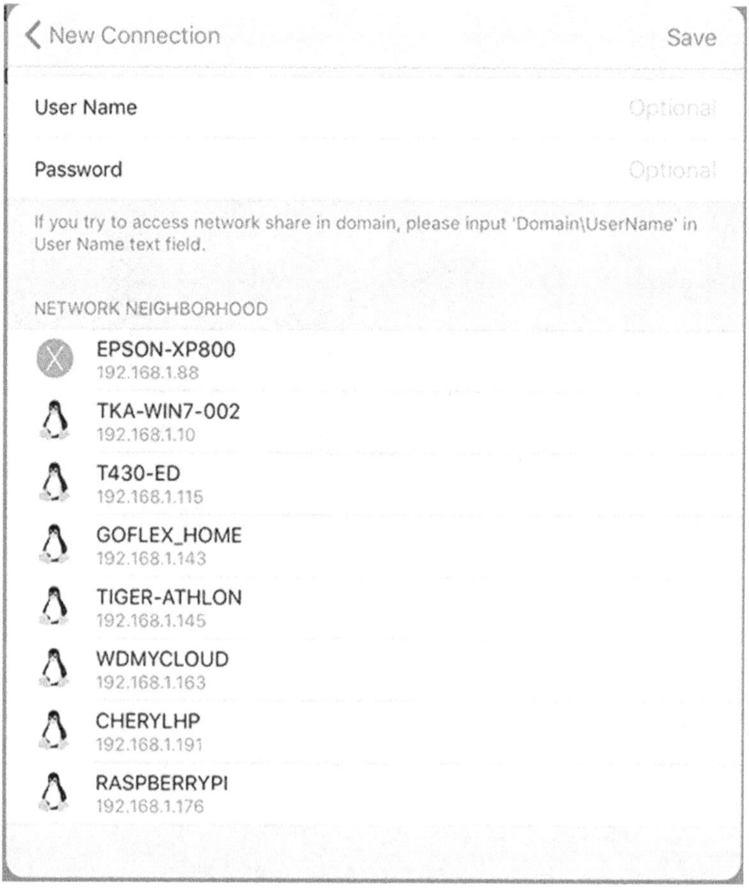

Figure 4-16. *Selecting from the remote user's home folder or the common share folder using Windows*

5. Click **Registered User** on the login dialog.

6. Enter your login name.

7. Enter your password.

8. Click **Login** (must login each time) or **Save & Login** (saves login information).

9. Click the shared folder you want to use.

Troubleshooting

If you cannot connect to a network share from a Raspberry Pi, make sure you have

- Configured the share settings properly

    - Connection type (smb or afp)

    - Username

    - Password

If you cannot connect to a Raspberry Pi share, make sure you have

- Created and properly configured a user share

    - Local user created

    - SMB user created

    - smb.conf syntax

Summary

Raspberry Pi uses Samba to connect to workgroup networks. Install Samba if it is not already installed. You can connect via a file manager or by using smbclient. Although wireless flash and hard drives are primarily intended for use with mobile devices, a Raspberry Pi can connect with them for read-only or read/write use, depending upon the specific drive in question. CUPS is used to connect to compatible network printers. SANE is used to connect to compatible network scanners. Use CUPS and SANE to connect to the printing and scanning functions of compatible multifunction devices.

CHAPTER 5

Sharing an Internet Connection

By using the Ethernet port found on most Raspberry Pi models to connect to a network and sharing that connection via wireless, you can provide a stronger signal to computers, printers, multifunction devices, and iOS or Android mobile devices that might otherwise be in "dead spots" for wireless coverage.

For devices that have wired network adapters only or have only outdated Wireless-G or older networking, you can use a wireless adapter on a Pi and share it via a network switch with computers or printers and multifunction devices.

Compared to a dedicated signal booster, the Raspberry Pi is much more versatile. It doesn't become useless if you install a router with a stronger wireless signal or run Ethernet cable. This chapter shows you how to share a wired or wireless connection.

Note The default wireless configuration for Raspbian Jessie with PIXEL is to receive an IP address from a DHCP server (typically a router). If you need to assign your Raspberry Pi a static IP address, you need to edit the dhcpcd.conf file. For details, see `www.modmypi.com/blog/how-to-give-your-raspberry-pi-a-static-ip-address-update`.

Hardware Used in This Chapter

- Raspberry Pi 3 OR
- Raspberry Pi 2 with Wi-Fi dongle OR
- Raspberry Pi Zero W
- Gigabit Ethernet (or Fast Ethernet) switch
- CAT5e cables
- Internet connection

© Mark Edward Soper 2017
M. E. Soper, *Expanding Your Raspberry Pi*, DOI 10.1007/978-1-4842-2922-4_5

Configuring the Pi for Sharing (Hardware)

In order to share an Internet connection with other devices, a Raspberry Pi needs two different network interfaces:

- A wired Ethernet (RJ-45) port

- A Wireless-N (802.11n) adapter

The Raspberry Pi 3 includes both, making it the best choice for sharing. However, if you have a Raspberry Pi 2, you have a wired Ethernet port and four USB ports, one of which can be used for a wireless dongle. The Raspberry Pi Zero W has the same wireless hardware as the Raspberry Pi 3, but has only one Micro-USB port. A wired USB to Ethernet adapter can be connected to that port.

■ **Caution**   If you want to share a wired connection using a wireless dongle, it must support Access Point or Master mode. Not all wireless dongles do. The official Raspberry Pi USB Wi-Fi dongle (www.raspberrypi.org/products/usb-wifi-dongle/) supports this mode. To learn about others, see http://elinux.org/RPi_USB_Wi-Fi_Adapters for test results. See also http://raspi.tv/2015/new-official-raspberry-pi-wifi-dongle-3-way-testing-vs-thepihut-and-edimax.

To determine the chipset used by a wireless adapter, use ethtool

```
sudo apt-get install ethtool
```

Ethtool -I displays driver (chipset) information. To see only the driver, use

```
ethtool -I wlanx |grep driver [x=1-4]
```

See www.raspberrypi.org/forums/viewtopic.php?t=159148&p=1034164 for details.

Configuring the Pi for Sharing (Software)

The packages needed for sharing your Raspberry Pi's Internet connection with other devices vary with the type of sharing you want to do. Typical packages used for sharing include

- hostapd (creates a virtual Wi-Fi access point [AP])

- hostap-utils (utilities used by hostapd)

- udhcpd (dhcp server; provides dynamic IP addresses)

- iw (configures wireless devices)

- `bridge-utils` (wireless bridging utilities)

- `dnsmasq` (DHCP server and DNS server)

- `network-manager` (manages network connections)

- `isc-dhcp-server` (dhcp server)

Many of these packages perform the same or similar tasks, so you will not need all of these in a particular configuration.

With any of these approaches, you will be editing configuration files for wired and wireless network connections, and, in some cases, for NAT (network address translation). Be sure to read carefully through the instructions before you start.

Planning the Network Configuration

No matter which type of Internet connection sharing you set up on your Pi, you might need to determine the range of IP addresses to allocate to clients. If you are using your Pi as an access point, you don't need to configure this setting, because the Pi is not used as a router or DHCP server. However, if you are using your Pi to share a wireless connection via an Ethernet port and switch with a separate network, you will need to assign a range of IP addresses that are not the same as those assigned by the existing DHCP and router.

For example, if the existing network uses addresses in the 192.168.1.xxx range, the Pi should assign addresses in the 192.168.2.xxx range. The networks will operate separately, but a network bridge enables the newly created 192.168.2.xxx range to connect with the existing network for Internet access.

To share a wired connection wirelessly, you also need to determine the following:

- 802.11 channel to use

- SSID to use

- WPA encryption type

- WPA encryption key/passphrase

To determine the 802.11 channel to use, use a Wi-Fi monitoring app or program. If you use an Android smartphone or tablet, you can use the Wifi Analyzer (Figure 5-1). The best channels to use with a 2.4GHz wireless adapter, such as the ones built into or designed for use with Raspberry Pi, are 1, 6, or 1l, as the other channels overlap with nearby channels.

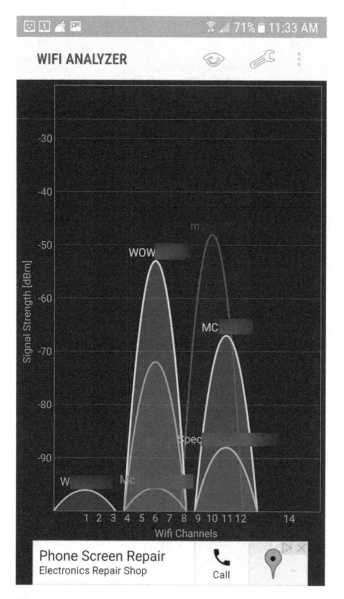

Figure 5-1. *In this example, channel 1 has the lowest level of interference from other wireless networks*

The SSID, which identifies your wireless network, can be any word or phrase you like. For best security, use an SSID which does not identify your ISP, your name, your location, or your device:

- **Bad SSID:** John'sPi_onMainSt_ABC_ISP

- **Good SSID:** AZ43098

The encryption type, which helps prevent wireless mooching by person or persons unknown, should be WPA2. The only reason to use the older WPA or first-generation, easily hacked WEP is if you are trying to share a connection with devices that should have gone to the boneyard years ago.

Finally, the encryption key should be a good mix of alphanumeric and punctuation characters (up to 60 characters):

- **Bad encryption key:** Mynetworkissafelhope

- **Good encryption key:** My-n07w0511#sa4e90-zz

Record the settings you plan to use, and you're ready to get started. For the configuration examples in this chapter, we will use the following settings. Be sure to change these as required for your network:

- Range of IP addresses to distribute with DHCP: 192.168.2.2-254 (or a subset)

- Static IP address to use for Pi as router: 192.168.2.1/255.255.255.0

- SSID: Some_Random_Name

- Encryption for wireless: WPA2

- WPA2 passphrase (key): T32t-1P@00Y

- 802.11n channel: 1

Sharing a Wired Connection Using a Wireless Adapter

In this scenario, the Raspberry Pi has an Internet connection via Ethernet and also has an on-board or USB wireless adapter. The Pi will be used as an access point for wireless devices to reach the Internet. By working as an access point, the original DHCP server provides IP addresses for the devices that connect to this access point as well to the ones that already connect to the router. Similarly, the original router provides network address translation (NAT) for the devices that connect via the access point as well as those that were already connected to the router. This configuration is considerably simpler than configurations that have the Raspberry Pi provide DHCP and NAT support.

This example is adapted from www.instructables.com/id/How-to-make-a-WiFi-Access-Point-out-of-a-Raspberry/. These directions have been updated for Raspbian Jessie.

■ **Tip** Commented lines start with a # symbol. I have added additional comments beyond the ones found in the source example to help further explain what the commands do.

Four packages are required:

- `hostapd`
- `hostap-utils`
- `iw`
- `bridge-utils`

■ **Tip** If you need to install more than one package at a time, you can use this syntax (replace package1, etc., with the actual package name): **sudo apt-get install package1 package2 package3**.

1. Connect your Raspberry Pi via an Ethernet cable and make sure you can connect to the Internet with it. For example, if you can get updates (Step 2), your Internet connection is working.

2. Update the list of packages:

   sudo apt-get update

3. Install the necessary software:

   sudo apt-get install hostapd hostap-utils iw bridge-utils

4. Open the hostapd file:

   sudo nano /etc/init.d/hostapd

5. Edit the line DAEMON_CONF= (see Figure 5-2):

   DAEMON_CONF=/etc/hostapd/hostapd.conf

```
#!/bin/sh

### BEGIN INIT INFO
# Provides:             hostapd
# Required-Start:       $remote_fs
# Required-Stop:        $remote_fs
# Should-Start:         $network
# Should-Stop:
# Default-Start:        2 3 4 5
# Default-Stop:         0 1 6
# Short-Description:    Advanced IEEE 802.11 management daemon
# Description:          Userspace IEEE 802.11 AP and IEEE 802.1X/WPA/WPA2/EAP
#                       Authenticator
### END INIT INFO

PATH=/sbin:/bin:/usr/sbin:/usr/bin
DAEMON_SBIN=/usr/sbin/hostapd
DAEMON_DEFS=/etc/default/hostapd
DAEMON_CONF=█

^G Get Help    ^O WriteOut    ^R Read File  ^Y Prev Page  ^K Cut Text   ^C Cur Pos
^X Exit        ^J Justify     ^W Where Is   ^V Next Page  ^U UnCut Text ^T To Spell
```

Figure 5-2. *The hostapd file before editing*

6. Save changes (Ctrl-O, press the Enter key) and exit (Ctrl-X) (see Figure 5-3).

```
#!/bin/sh

/etc/hostapd/hostapd.conf### BEGIN INIT INFO
# Provides:             hostapd
# Required-Start:       $remote_fs
# Required-Stop:        $remote_fs
# Should-Start:         $network
# Should-Stop:
# Default-Start:        2 3 4 5
# Default-Stop:         0 1 6
# Short-Description:    Advanced IEEE 802.11 management daemon
# Description:          Userspace IEEE 802.11 AP and IEEE 802.1X/WPA/WPA2/EAP
#                       Authenticator
### END INIT INFO

PATH=/sbin:/bin:/usr/sbin:/usr/bin
DAEMON_SBIN=/usr/sbin/hostapd
DAEMON_DEFS=/etc/default/hostapd
DAEMON_CONF=/etc/hostapd/hostapd.conf█      I
                      [ Wrote 67 lines ]
^G Get Help    ^O WriteOut    ^R Read File  ^Y Prev Page  ^K Cut Text   ^C Cur Pos
^X Exit        ^J Justify     ^W Where Is   ^V Next Page  ^U UnCut Text ^T To Spell
```

Figure 5-3. *The hostapd file after editing*

7. Create hostapd.conf. If the file does not already exist, the following command opens up a blank file:

    sudo nano /etc/hostapd/hostapd.conf

8.   Add the following to the hostapd.conf file:

```
ctrl_interface=/var/run/hostapd
################################
# Basic Config
################################
macaddr_acl=0 auth_algs=1
# Most modern wireless drivers in the kernel need driver=nl80211
driver=nl80211
##########################
# Local configuration...
##########################
interface=wlan0
bridge=br0
hw_mode=g
ieee80211n=1
channel=1 #Use a channel that is the least congested
ssid=Some_Random_Name #Not the same as your existing WLAN's SSID
macaddr_acl=0
auth_algs=1
ignore_broadcast_ssid=0
wpa=3
wpa_passphrase=T32t-1P@OOY #Replace with your preferred
passphrase
wpa_key_mgmt=WPA-PSK
#wpa_pairwise=TKIP #Uncomment this line to support WPA encryption
rsn_pairwise=CCMP #This line supports WPA2 encryption
### Following recommended for use with R Pi 3 or Pi Zero W's
onboard Wi-Fi
wmm_enabled=1          # QoS support
ht_capab=[HT40][SHORT-GI-20][DSSS_CCK-40]
#[HT40]support for 20 and 40MHz channels
#[SHORT-GI-20]support for short guard interval for 20MHz channels
#[DSSS_CCK-40]support for 40MHz data rates
```

■ **Note** Step 8 provides the instructions to create a WPA2-secured network. You can also set up an open (unsecured) network in this step by omitting the lines that begin with wpa=, wpa_passphrase=, wpa_key_mgmt=, rsn_pairwise=, and wpa_pairwise=.

---

9.   Save changes (Ctrl-O, press the Enter key) and exit(Ctrl-X).

10.   Open the /etc/network/interfaces file:

sudo nano /etc/network/interfaces

11. Configure the network bridge by adding the following lines to the beginning of the file if not already present:

```
auto lo
iface lo inet loopback
auto br0 #br0 is the bridge
iface br0 inet static
address 192.168.1.11
netmask 255.255.255.0
network 192.168.1.0
broadcast 192.168.1.255
gateway 192.168.1.1
bridge-ports eth0 wlan0 #bridges the Ethernet port to Wi-Fi
```

12. Save changes (Ctrl-O, press the Enter key) and exit (Ctrl-X).

13. Reboot the Raspberry Pi. When you log back in, your repeater should be running and ready to extend your network.

Sharing a Wireless Connection Using an Ethernet Port and Switch

If you want to create a separate network that can still access the Internet, you can share a Raspberry Pi's wireless network by using its built-in Ethernet port along with an Ethernet switch. Because you are connecting two networks together, you will need to create routing tables on the Pi. The following is based on https://raspberrypi.stackexchange.com/questions/48307/sharing-the-pis-wifi-connection-through-the-ethernet-port. I have added illustrations, comments, and clarifications.

One package needs to be installed:

- dnsmasq

Files to edit:

- /etc/network/interfaces (configures wireless and Ethernet interfaces)

- /etc/dnsmasq.conf (configures dns masquerading)

- /etc/sysctl.conf (enables packet forwarding)

- /etc/iptables (via save commands from command line, not nano; configures IP routing tables)

- /etc/rc.local (restores routing tables)

1. Connect an Ethernet switch to the RPi's Ethernet port with a standard CAT5e or better cable (not a crossover cable). The Pi's Ethernet port supports 10/100Mbps Ethernet speeds, so a Fast Ethernet switch is sufficient. However, a Gigabit Ethernet switch (10/100/1000Mbps) is also suitable.

2. Connect a second Ethernet cable between the switch and a PC.

3. Start the RPi and log into it.

4. Enter **sudo apt-get update**.

5. Enter **sudo apt-get install dnsmasq**.

6. Use **sudo nano /etc/network/interfaces** to edit the interfaces file. If you prefer a different editor, substitute it for nano in the commands in this section.

7. Add these lines to the eth0 section:

    ```
    allow-hotplug eth0
    iface eth0 inet static
        address 192.168.2.1
        netmask 255.255.255.0
        network 192.168.2.0
        broadcast 192.168.2.255
    ```

8. Save changes and exit (Ctrl-O, press the Enter key, and Ctrl-X).

9. Move the original dnsmasq.conf file:

    sudo mv /etc/dnsmasq.conf /etc/dnsmasq.conf.orig

10. Create and edit a new (blank) version of dnsmasq.conf:

    sudo nano /etc/dnsmasq.conf

11. Add the following lines (# indicates an optional comment; see Figure 5-4):

    ```
    interface=eth0        # Use interface eth0
    listen-address=192.168.2.1 # listen on
    # Bind to the interface to make sure we aren't sending things
    # elsewhere
    bind-interfaces
    server=8.8.8.8        # Forward DNS requests to Google DNS
    server=8.8.4.4        # Secondary Google DNS server
    domain-needed         # Don't forward short names
    # Never forward addresses in the nonrouted address spaces.
    bogus-priv
    # Assign IP addresses between 192.168.2.2 and 192.168.2.100 with a
    # 12 hour lease time
    dhcp-range=192.168.2.2,192.168.2.100,12h
    ```

```
  GNU nano 2.2.6              File: /etc/dnsmasq.conf

interface=eth0      # Use interface eth0
listen-address=192.168.2.1 # listen on
# Bind to the interface to make sure we aren't sending things
# elsewhere
bind-interfaces
server=8.8.8.8        # Forward DNS requests to Google DNS
server=8.8.4.4        # If primary Google DNS server doesn't respond, this Google server will be used
domain-needed         # Don't forward short names
# Never forward addresses in the non-routed address spaces.
bogus-priv
# Assign IP addresses between 192.168.2.2 and 192.168.2.100 with a
# 12 hour lease time
dhcp-range=192.168.2.2,192.168.2.100,12h
█




                           [ Read 13 lines ]
^G Get Help    ^O WriteOut    ^R Read File    ^Y Prev Page    ^K Cut Text     ^C Cur Pos
^X Exit        ^J Justify     ^W Where Is     ^V Next Page    ^U UnCut Text   ^T To Spell
```

Figure 5-4. *The dnsmasq.conf file after editing*

12.   Save changes and exit (Ctrl-O, press the Enter key, and Ctrl-X).

■ **Note**   The original version of this file didn't include a second DNS server. Having at least two DNS servers is good practice, as the secondary server will be used if the primary server fails.

---

13.   Edit the /etc/sysctl.conf file to enable packet forwarding:

sudo nano /etc/sysctl.conf

14.   Remove the # from the beginning of the line containing net. ipv4.ip_forward=1. The line before editing:

```
#net.ipv4.ip_forward=1
```

The line after editing:

```
net.ipv4.ip_forward=1
```

15.   Network address translation (NAT) is used to connect the wireless LAN (wlan0) on the Raspberry Pi with the devices that connect via Ethernet (eth0) and a switch. Use the following command to set up NAT:

sudo iptables -t nat -A POSTROUTING -o wlan0 -j MASQUERADE

sudo iptables -A FORWARD -i wlan0 -o eth0 -m state --state RELATED,ESTABLISHED -j ACCEPT

sudo iptables -A FORWARD -i eth0 -o wlan0 -j ACCEPT

▨ Tip   iptables terms and syntax to know

POSTROUTING: altering packets as they leave

MASQUERADE: used for network address translation (NAT)

FORWARD: sending data

RELATED: new connection from a packet that is associated with an existing connection

ESTABLISHED: data packet is associated with a connection that has sent and received data

ACCEPT: packet allowed through

-j: jumps to specified action (a.k.a. "target") when packet matches a particular rule

-t: specifies table name

-o: outgoing network interface to use for a rule

-A: appends iptable to end of specified chain of rules

-m: loads match option module by specified name

-I: specifies the network interface used for incoming traffic

---

16.   The following command creates a file that saves the rules for reuse:

sudo sh -c "iptables-save > /etc/iptables.ipv4.nat"

17.   To enable the rules to be used automatically when the system reboots, edit /etc/rc.local and add `iptables-restore < /etc/iptables.ipv4.nat` near the end of the file:

sudo nano /etc/rc.local

End of file before editing:

`exit 0`

End of file after editing:

```
iptables-restore < /etc/iptables.ipv4.nat
exit 0
```

18.   Restart the Raspberry Pi:

sudo reboot

19. After rebooting, you can view the routing tables (Figure 5-5) with **route**

```
pi@raspberrypi:~ $ route
Kernel IP routing table
Destination     Gateway          Genmask          Flags Metric Ref    Use Iface
default         192.168.1.1      0.0.0.0          UG    303    0        0 wlan0
link-local      *                255.255.0.0      U     202    0        0 eth0
192.168.1.0     *                255.255.255.0    U     303    0        0 wlan0
192.168.2.0     *                255.255.255.0    U     0      0        0 eth0
pi@raspberrypi:~ $ ▮
```

Figure 5-5. *A properly configured routing table. The Raspberry Pi's wireless (wlan0) connection is using the 192.168.1.x range, while the Ethernet (eth0) connection is usig the 192.168.2.x range.*

20. To test the connection, use the PC connected to the second Ethernet cable and run a ping command such as **ping 192.168.2.1** (Figure 5-6):

```
🖥 Command Prompt                                         —     □     ✕

Microsoft Windows [Version 10.0.14393]
(c) 2016 Microsoft Corporation. All rights reserved.

C:\Users\Mark>ping 192.168.2.1

Pinging 192.168.2.1 with 32 bytes of data:
Reply from 192.168.2.1: bytes=32 time<1ms TTL=64
Reply from 192.168.2.1: bytes=32 time<1ms TTL=64
Reply from 192.168.2.1: bytes=32 time=15ms TTL=64
Reply from 192.168.2.1: bytes=32 time<1ms TTL=64

Ping statistics for 192.168.2.1:
    Packets: Sent = 4, Received = 4, Lost = 0 (0% loss),
Approximate round trip times in milli-seconds:
    Minimum = 0ms, Maximum = 15ms, Average = 3ms

C:\Users\Mark>
```

Figure 5-6. *A successful ping command receives replies back from the IP address set up on the Raspberry Pi for sharing*

Troubleshooting

To help prevent (and fix) problems you might encounter when working with existing or new procedures for Internet sharing, keep the following tips in mind:

- Use ipconfig or ifconfig to check IP addresses on your client PCs. If a system that is supposed to get an IP address from a DHCP server (router or Raspberry Pi) has a 169.254.x.x address, it is not receiving an IP address. Run ifconfig on the Raspberry Pi to determine if it is properly configured.

- Use route to view the routing tables created by iptables. If you don't see results similar to those in Figure 5-5, odds are you won't be able to connect to the Internet. Recheck your file commands for eth0, wlan0, and bridging.

- A bad Ethernet port or cable can cause sharing to fail. Look for activity lights on each cable connected to a Raspberry Pi or device that is active. Lack of activity lights suggests a problem. Swap ports or cables to find the problem. Keep in mind that both ends of the cable need to be connected to running devices to display activity lights.

Tip   Understanding Autoconfiguration addresses

The 169.254.x.x address is an autoconfiguration address that is used only if a system set to receive an IP address automatically cannot connect to a DHCP server. Compare existing IP address ranges and make sure that the Raspberry Pi is using a different IP address range. Also, be sure to check switch and cable power and connections.

Summary

To share an Internet connection, your Raspberry Pi needs both a wireless adapter and an Ethernet port. The Raspberry Pi 3 has both, but with most other models, you will need to add a wireless adapter. The Pi Zero has neither type of adapter, while the Pi Zero W has a wireless adapter, but no Ethernet port.

Depending upon whether you are sharing a wireless or wired connection, you can use a variety of packages available for Raspbian Jessie (PIXEL or Lite versions).

Before you start, plan your network configuration by determining the IP address range(s) already in use on your network. If you are sharing a wired connection wirelessly, you also need to determine wireless settings to use, such as 802.11 channel, SSID, and encryption settings.

If you want to share a wireless connection, your Raspberry Pi will need not only an Ethernet port (or USB to Ethernet adapter), but also an Ethernet switch.

CHAPTER 6

Setting Up a Print and Scan Server

To turn your Raspberry Pi into a print and scan server, you need to perform the following tasks, all of which are covered in this chapter:

- Connect your printer, scanner, or multifunction (print/scan/copy) device to your Raspberry Pi

- Install and configure CUPS (Common Unix Print Service) on your Raspberry Pi

- Create users that can connect remotely to a CUPS printer

- Install and configure SANE (Scanner Access Now Easy) on your Raspberry Pi

- Create users that can connect remotely to a SANE scanner

- Install CUPS or SANE clients (if necessary) to remote systems that will connect to the printer, scanner, or multifunction device

There is also an optional task:

- Configuring the Raspberry Pi for headless booting and remote control with SSH

Hardware Used in This Chapter

- A multifunction unit (print/scanner/copier)

- Raspberry Pi Node Zero (or other Raspberry Pi model using flash memory or a hard disk [recommended])

© Mark Edward Soper 2017

M. E. Soper, *Expanding Your Raspberry Pi*, DOI 10.1007/978-1-4842-2922-4_6

Connecting via USB

Most printers or multifunction (print/scan/copy) devices connect via USB. However, unlike Windows or MacOS (OSX), which can automatically detect USB devices, you must manually configure a printer or multifunction device after you connect it to your Raspberry Pi.

■ **Caution**   Boot your computer, log into it, and then connect your printer or multifunction device. If you connect the printer/device first, you could cause a kernel panic because Raspbian or other OSes will try to read the USB port or card reader.

If you use a Raspberry Pi Zero, ZeroW, 1, or 1+, you have only one USB port. If you need more than one USB port (for example, for a wireless or wired network adapter or a USB drive), be sure to choose a supported USB hub that has its own power supply. See http://elinux.org/RPi_Powered_USB_Hubs for a large list of tested hubs.

■ **Caution**   Some powered USB hubs can use one USB port to power some Raspberry Pi models. Be sure to review the notes on the eLinux page listed in the preceding paragraph to determine which hubs can do this.

Selecting a Distro

To reduce computing overhead and space requirements, it makes sense to use a GUI-less Linux distro such as Raspbian Jessie Lite for your print and scan server.

■ **Note**   Because of the limited lifespan of flash memory cards when used for frequent writes, I recommend installing Raspbian Jessie Lite or other Linux distros to a hard disk drive. I used the Pi Node Zero from WDLabs, which features a low-power 2.5-inch WD hard disk drive and a built-in two-port USB hub. For more information about using Pi Node Zero and other hard disks with Raspberry Pi, see Chapter 3.

Manual Connections to a Wireless Network

To install CUPS, Samba, and drivers for your printer and scanner, you need to connect to the Internet.

If you use a wireless network, it might be necessary to manually configure Raspbian Jessie Lite to use it. Here are two clues that your system doesn't have a working wireless connection:

- Running an apt-get command results in errors (Figure 6-1)

```
pi@raspberrypi:~ $ sudo apt-get update
Err http://archive.raspberrypi.org jessie InRelease

Err http://mirrordirector.raspbian.org jessie InRelease

Err http://archive.raspberrypi.org jessie Release.gpg
  Temporary failure resolving 'archive.raspberrypi.org'
Err http://mirrordirector.raspbian.org jessie Release.gpg
  Temporary failure resolving 'mirrordirector.raspbian.org'
Reading package lists... Done
W: Failed to fetch http://mirrordirector.raspbian.org/raspbian/dists/jessie/InRelease

W: Failed to fetch http://archive.raspberrypi.org/debian/dists/jessie/InRelease
```

Figure 6-1. *Errors such as **Temporary failure resolving...** or **Failed to fetch** while running an apt-get command indicate a lack of a network connection*

- ifconfig doesn't display a valid address for your wireless adapter (Figure 6-2)

```
pi@raspberrypi:~ $ sudo ifconfig
lo        Link encap:Local Loopback
          inet addr:127.0.0.1  Mask:255.0.0.0
          inet6 addr: ::1/128 Scope:Host
          UP LOOPBACK RUNNING  MTU:65536  Metric:1
          RX packets:672 errors:0 dropped:0 overruns:0 frame:0
          TX packets:672 errors:0 dropped:0 overruns:0 carrier:0
          collisions:0 txqueuelen:1
          RX bytes:54560 (53.2 KiB)  TX bytes:54560 (53.2 KiB)

wlan0     Link encap:Ethernet  HWaddr d4:7b:b0:7a:20:64
          inet6 addr: fe80::c750:84b6:aadd:13f0/64 Scope:Link
          UP BROADCAST MULTICAST  MTU:1500  Metric:1
          RX packets:5956 errors:0 dropped:1881 overruns:0 frame:0
          TX packets:0 errors:0 dropped:0 overruns:0 carrier:0
          collisions:0 txqueuelen:1000
          RX bytes:783262 (764.9 KiB)  TX bytes:0 (0.0 B)
```

Figure 6-2. *wlan0 has no IPv4 (inet) address, indicating it has no network connection*

To set up a wireless configuration, follow these steps:

1. Open the wpa_supplicant.conf file for editing [nano is the default text editor]:

   sudo nano /etc/wpa_supplicant/wpa_supplicant.conf

2. Add the following statements to the end of the file (use your actual SSID and encryption key in place of the placeholders):

   ```
   network={
       ssid="YourSSID"
       psk="YourEncryptionKey"
   }
   ```

3. To save changes, press Ctrl-X, then Y when prompted.

4. Reboot: **sudo reboot**.

5. After rebooting, run **sudo ifconfig wlan0** to verify that you now have a working Internet connection (Figure 6-3).

```
pi@raspberrypi:~ $ ifconfig wlan0
wlan0     Link encap:Ethernet  HWaddr d4:7b:b0:7a:20:64
          inet addr:192.168.1.154  Bcast:192.168.1.255  Mask:255.255.255.0
          inet6 addr: fe80::c750:84b6:aadd:13f0/64 Scope:Link
          UP BROADCAST RUNNING MULTICAST  MTU:1500  Metric:1
          RX packets:86 errors:0 dropped:25 overruns:0 frame:0
          TX packets:69 errors:0 dropped:0 overruns:0 carrier:0
          collisions:0 txqueuelen:1000
          RX bytes:15694 (15.3 KiB)  TX bytes:8633 (8.4 KiB)
```

Figure 6-3. After rebooting, wlan0 now has a valid IPv4 (inet) address received from the DHCP server in the wireless router

6. Be sure to note the IP(v4) address of your Raspberry Pi. In Figure 6-3, it is 192.168.1.154. You will use the Pi's IP address to connect to CUPS remotely.

Installing and Using CUPS

After verifying that you have a working Internet connection, the next step is to update your system and install CUPS:

```
sudo apt-get update
sudo apt-get install cups
```

▪ **Note** Depending upon the printer or multifunction unit you use, CUPS might already include drivers for your device, or you might need to add drivers. See "Installing Printer Drivers," in this chapter for details.

Adding Users to the Print Administration Group

Unless you add your account to the Print Administration group, the only user that can administer print jobs would be root (su). Switch to the root (su) account with sudo su and use the usermod command to add your user account (pi) to the group:

usermod -a -G lpadmin pi

To view the groups a particular user (pi) belongs to:

groups pi

Figure 6-4 illustrates the groups user pi belongs to before and after using usermod.

```
pi@raspberrypi:~ $ groups
pi adm dialout cdrom sudo audio video plugdev games users input netdev gpio i2c spi
pi@raspberrypi:~ $ sudo su
root@raspberrypi:/home/pi# usermod -a -G lpadmin pi
root@raspberrypi:/home/pi# groups pi
pi : pi adm dialout cdrom sudo audio video plugdev games users input netdev spi i2c gpio lpadmin
root@raspberrypi:/home/pi#
```

Figure 6-4. *Adding the user pi to the lpadmin group*

To return to the normal user account, enter the command **exit**.

Configuring CUPS for Remote Administration

The next step in setting up a printer is to run CUPS to name the printer and install the appropriate printer driver. However, CUPS is configured from a web browser. By editing the CUPS configuration file (cupsd.conf), we can allow remote administration via another computer's web browser:

sudo nano/etc/cups/cupsd.conf

Make the following changes:

- Replace `Listen localhost: 631` with `Port 631`

- In the sections headed <Location />, <Location /admin>, <Location /admin/conf>, add the line

    `Allow @local after the line Order allow, deny`

Save changes by pressing Ctrl-X, Y.
Restart with

sudo service cups restart

Logging into CUPS Remotely

If you are using an older printer or multifunction device, it's likely that CUPS already has a suitable printer driver. In this section, you learn how to log into CUPS from a remote computer's web browser, select a printer, and configure it.

To connect to your Raspberry Pi from another computer on the network:

1. Open a web browser.

2. Enter the Pi's IP(v4) address (replace the xxx in the following example with the actual number) and port number into the browser window: `xxx.xxx.xxx.xxx:631`.

3. The CUPS home tab appears (Figure 6-5).

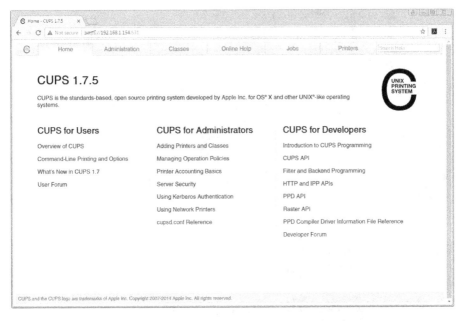

Figure 6-5. *Logging into CUPS remotely*

Selecting and Configuring a Printer with CUPS

After opening CUPS, click Adding Printers and Classes to start the printer selection process:

1. Click the local printer

2. Click **Continue** (Figure 6-6)

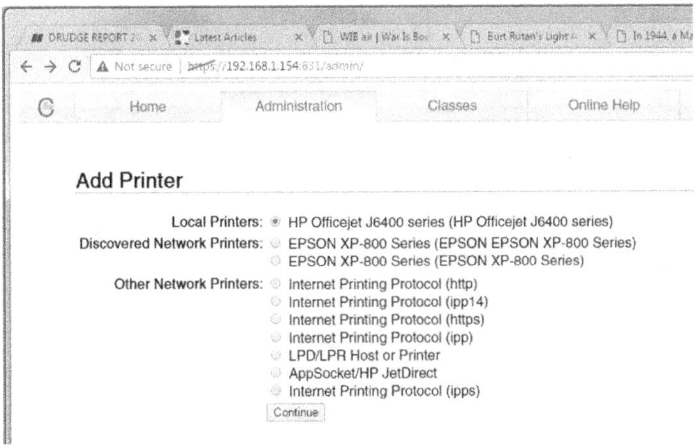

Figure 6-6. *Starting the Add Printer process*

3. On the next dialog, enter the location (optional)

4. Click the empty **Share This Printer** box to check it

5. Click **Continue** (Figure 6-7)

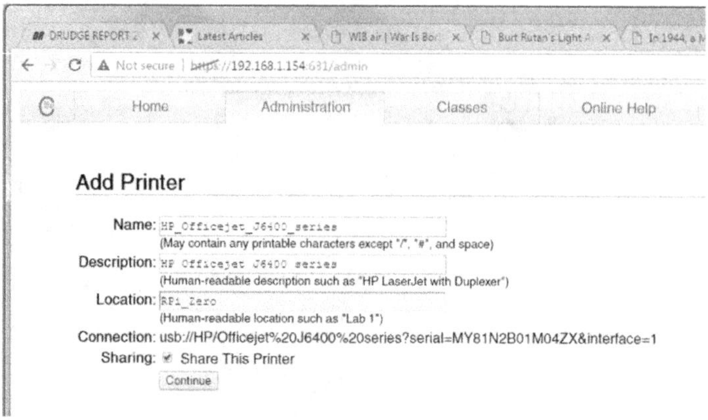

Figure 6-7. *Specifying the location and enabling printer sharing*

6. Select the printer make (if not already selected) and model

7. Click **Add Printer** (Figure 6-8)

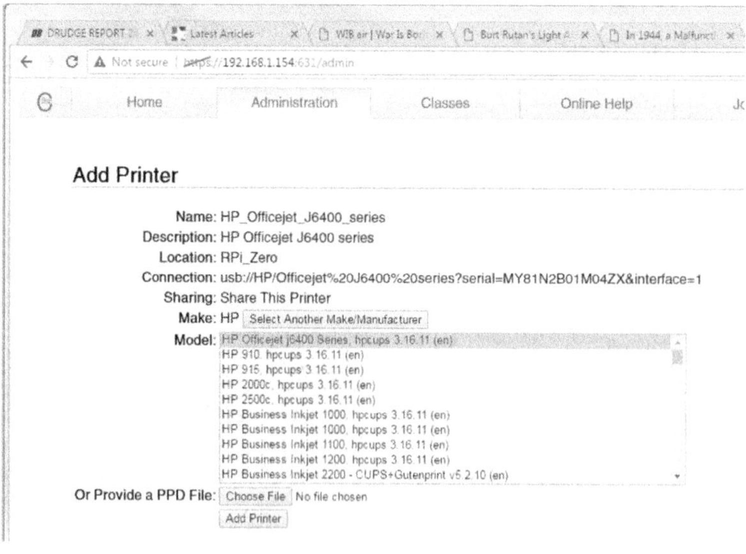

Figure 6-8. *Adding the printer*

Note If you do not find your printer model, you have two options: select a similar model and see if it works by creating a document and printing it, or download and install the correct printer driver (next section) and rerun CUPS afterward.

8.   Select the options desired for the printer, such as the default paper size, media type, and print quality (Figure 6-9) on the General tab.

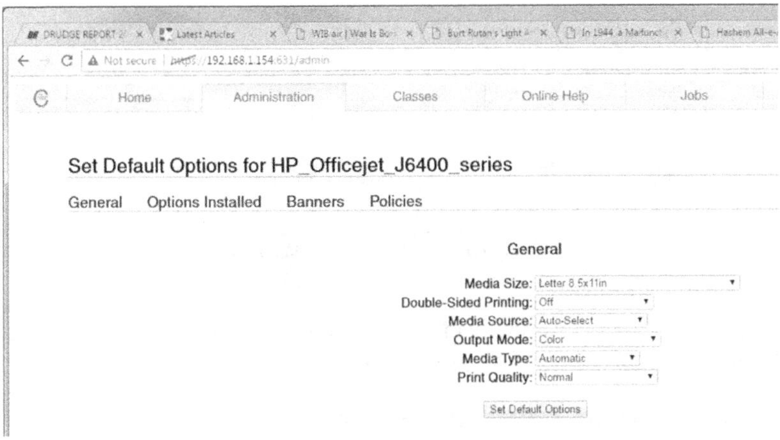

Figure 6-9. *Setting default options for the printer*

9.   Click other tabs to set up all desired options.

10.   Click **Set Default Options** when you are finished.

Installing Printer Drivers

If your printer or multifunction device is not listed in CUPS and a satisfactory substitute driver is not available, you need to download the correct driver.

Note To support a multifunction device for printing and scanning, you need to use CUPS (for printing) and SANE (for scanning). See "Installing and Configuring SANE," in this chapter.

To search for printer drivers to install, use the apt-cache search command (replace printerdriver with the actual brand of printer):

```
sudo apt-cache search printerdriver
```

■ **Note**   apt-cache can also be used to display details of a particular package (sudo apt-cache show pkgname) or dependencies (sudo apt-cache showpkg pkgname). For more information, see www.tecmint.com/useful-basic-commands-of-apt-get-and-apt-cache-for-package-management/.

In Figure 6-10, I searched for an Epson printer driver with **sudo apt-cache epson**. The search located several utility packages as well as the actual Epson printer driver I needed.

```
pi@raspberrypi:~ $ sudo apt-cache search epson
escputil - maintenance utility for Epson Stylus printers
libimage-exiftool-perl - library and program to read and write meta information in multimedia files
libinklevel-dev - development files for libinklevel5
libinklevel5 - library for checking the ink level of your local printer
mtink - Status monitor tool for Epson inkjet printers
mtink-doc - Status monitor tool for Epson inkjet printers - documentation
photopc - Interface to digital still cameras
printer-driver-escpr - printer driver for Epson Inkjet that use ESC/P-R
pi@raspberrypi:~ $
```

Figure 6-10. *Searching for printer drivers and utiliies with the **apt-cache search** command*

To install the printer driver, use this command replace printer-driver-yourprinter with the actual printer driver file name):

sudo apt-get install printer-driver-yourprinter

■ **Tip**   For most HP printers and multifunction devices, download and install HPLIP (the HP Linux Printing and Imaging system).

Installing and Configuring Samba

To enable your Raspberry Pi to receive print and scan jobs, install and configure Samba, which provides SMB/CIFS file and print support to network clients running Windows, Linux, or MacOS (OSX) operating systems. Installing Samba is easy:

sudo apt-get install samba

After Samba is installed, use this command to open and edit its configuration files:

sudo nano /etc/samba/smb.conf

Make the following changes to the [global] section (replace Workgroup_name with the actual name of your workgroup) and add the security = user command:

```
workgroup = Workgroup_name
    ...
security = user
```

In the [printers] section make sure the browseable and guest OK settings are set to yes:

```
browsable = yes
guest ok = yes
```

Press Ctrl-X, Y to exit and save changes. To complete the process, restart Samba:

sudo /etc/init.d/samba restart

The default Samba configuration will automatically share any printers installed.

Connecting to a Samba Print Server with Windows

To connect to a Samba print server using Windows 7:

1. Open Control Panel.

2. Click **View Devices and Printers**.

3. Click **Add a printer**.

4. Click **Add a network, wireless, or Bluetooth printer** (Figure 6-11).

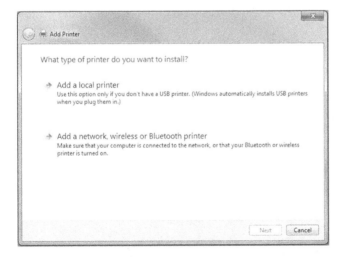

Figure 6-11. *Searching for a network printer*

5. Click **Next**.

6. Select the printer (Figure 6-12).

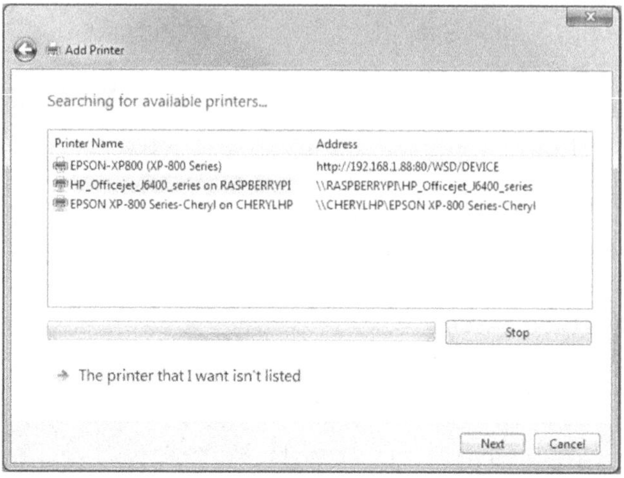

Figure 6-12. *Selecting the network printer*

7. Click **Next**.

8. Click **OK** on the No driver found alert.

9. Select the printer name and model from the Add Printer
    Wizard dialog (Figure 6-13).

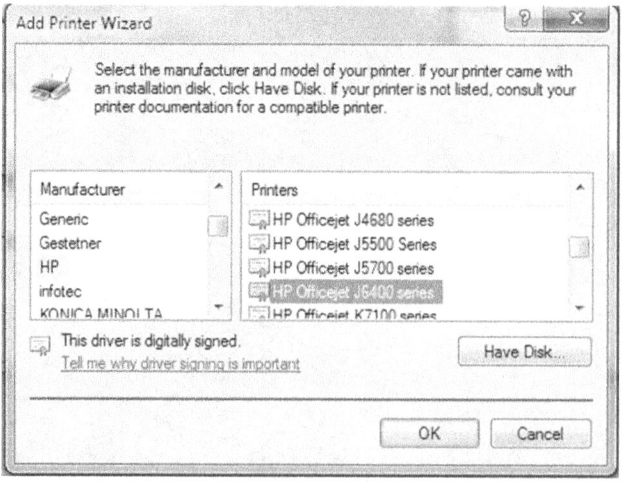

Figure 6-13. *Selecting the printer driver*

10. Click **OK**.

11. Click **Next**.

12. If you want to use this printer as the default, click the **Set as the default printer** check box (Figure 6-14).

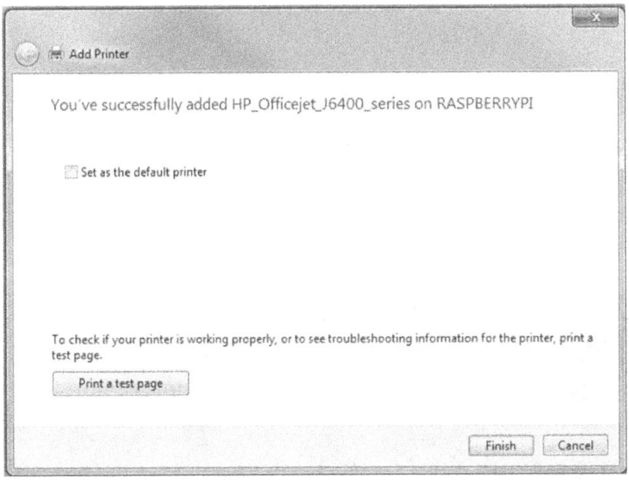

Figure 6-14. *Finishing printer setup*

13. Click **Print a test page**.

14. Click **Close**.

15. Click **Finish**.

To connect to a Samba print server using Windows 8.1 or 10:

1. Open **Settings**.

2. Click **Devices**.

3. Click **Printers & scanners**.

4. Click **Add a printer or scanner** (Figure 6-15).

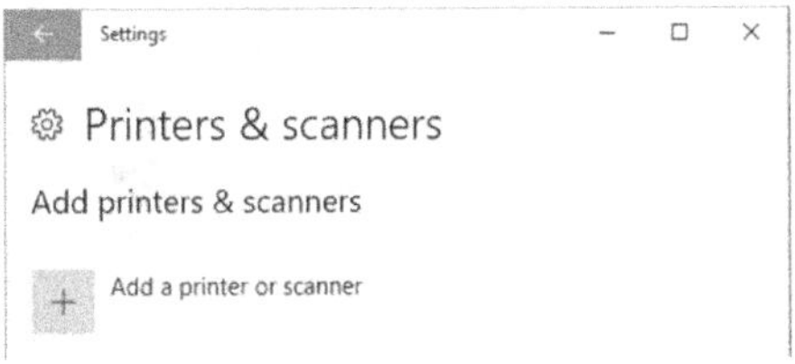

Figure 6-15. *Starting the Add a printer process in Windows 10*

111

5.   Click **The printer that I want isn't listed**.

6.   Click **Select a shared printer by name**.

7.   Click **Browse**.

8.   Click the Raspberry Pi (default name **RASPBERRYPI**), then click **Select**.

9.   Click your printer, then click **Select**.

10. Click **Next** (Figure 6-16).

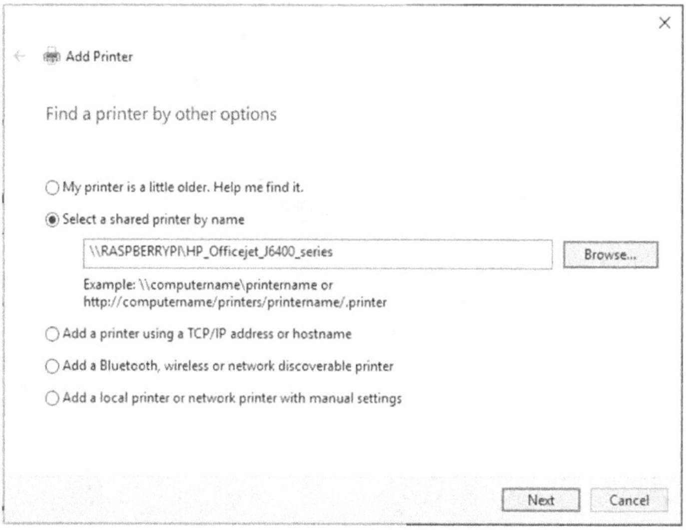

Figure 6-16. Selecting the printer by name

11. Click **OK** on the No driver found alert.

12. Continue with Steps 8-14 from the Windows 7 instructions. Close Settings after you are finished.

■ **Note**   If your printer is not listed in the Add Printer Wizard dialog, quit the process, download and install the appropriate printer driver, and restart the process. With some printers, you might need to connect the printer to your Windows computer to install the driver. After the driver is installed, you can disconnect the printer, delete the printer, and reconnect the printer to your Raspberry Pi. You can then follow these instructions to install the printer as a network printer.

Connecting to a Samba Print Server with MacOS (OSX)

Connecting to a Samba print server with MacOS (OSX) is a lot simpler than it is in Windows:

    1.   Click System Preferences (Figure 6-17)

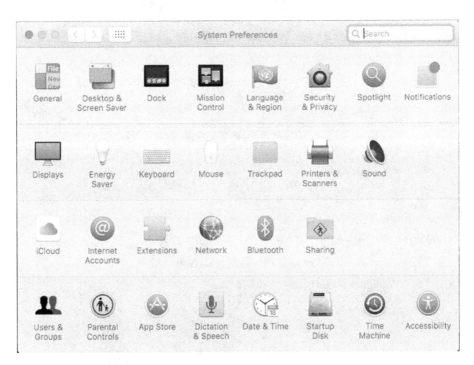

Figure 6-17. *Opening System Preferences*

    2.   Click Printers and Scanners

    3.   Click the + (Plus) sign in the Printers window (Figure 6-18)

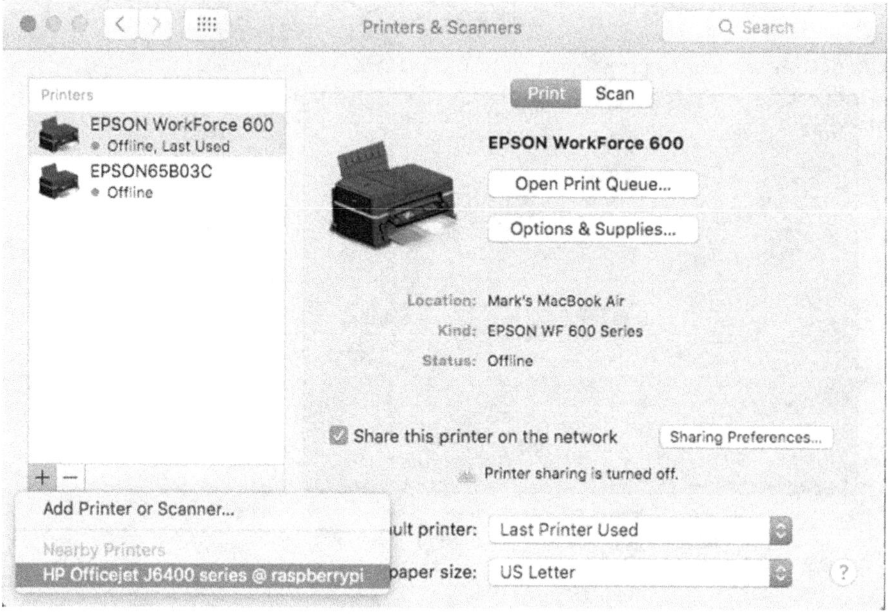

Figure 6-18. Selecting the printer hosted on the Raspberry Pi

4. Click the printer attached to the Raspberry Pi

5. Configure the printer (Figure 6-19)

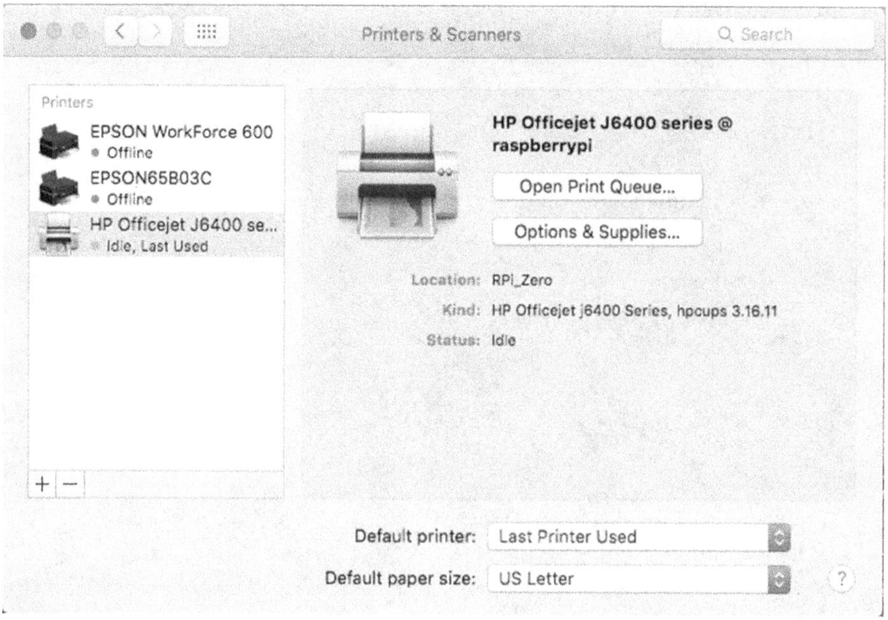

Figure 6-19. Configuring the printer

Installing and Configuring SANE

Most printers are actually multifunction devices (print, scan, copy, etc.). To enable a Raspberry Pi to be used as a scanner server (using the scanner function of the device, or a dedicated scanner), install SANE (Scanner Access Now Easy):

```
sudo apt-get update
sudo apt-get install sane
```

To determine if your scanner is detected, run `sane-find-scanner`:

```
sudo sane-find-scanner
```

Figure 6-20 illustrates the output from my system. It's normal, by the way, for this command to find other USB devices, such as a USB wireless adapter. Note the location of the scanner (libusb:001:007). We will need to use this information later to complete scanner setup.

```
pi@raspberrypi:~ $ sudo sane-find-scanner

  # sane-find-scanner will now attempt to detect your scanner. If the
  # result is different from what you expected, first make sure your
  # scanner is powered up and properly connected to your computer.

  # No SCSI scanners found. If you expected something different, make sure that
  # you have loaded a kernel SCSI driver for your SCSI adapter.

found USB scanner (vendor=0x03f0 [HP], product=0x3312 [Officejet J6400 series])
  libusb:001:007
found USB scanner (vendor=0x0a5c [Broadcom], product=0xbd1e [BCMUSB 802.11
  Adapter]) at libusb:001:006
could not fetch string descriptor: Pipe error
  # Your USB scanner was (probably) detected. It may or may not be supported by
  # SANE. Try scanimage -L and read the backend's manpage.

  # Not checking for parallel port scanners.

  # Most Scanners connected to the parallel port or other proprietary ports
  # can't be detected by this program.
pi@raspberrypi:~ $
```

Figure 6-20. *Using* `sane-find-scanner` *to locate the installed scanner or multifunction device*

To determine if scanimage (the scanning utility built into SANE) can use the scanner, run

```
sudo scanimage -L
```

Available scanners are identified (Figure 6-21).

```
pi@raspberrypi:~ $ sudo scanimage -L
device `epson2:net:192.168.1.88' is a Epson PID 089B flatbed scanner
device `hpaio:/usb/Officejet_J6400_series?serial=MY81N2B01M04ZX' is a
  Hewlett-Packard Officejet_J6400_series all-in-one
pi@raspberrypi:~ $
```

Figure 6-21. *Using* scanimage -L *to locate available scanners. The Epson all-in-one device is available via the network, and the HP Officejet is connected to the Raspberry Pi via a USB port.*

■ **Tip** If scanimage -L detects two or more scanners (see Figure 6-21), edit the dll.conf file used by SANE to support scanners: **sudo nano /etc/sane.d/dll.conf**. Place a # in front of the scanner brand(s) that you do **not** want to use. After saving your changes and exiting, run **sudo scanimage -L** again. This time, only one scanner should be listed.

To test the scanner, insert a document or photo and use one of the following commands:

- **sudo scanimage >test.tiff** (this creates a TIF file that can be used with Windows, MacOS/OSX, and Linux apps)

- **sudo scanimage >test.pnm** (this creates a file that can be used by the open source GIMP image editor)

Configuring SANE as a Server

To configure SANE to run as a server, we need to edit two files that control how SANE works, saned and saned.conf:

Edit saned with sudo nano /etc/default/saned

- Change Run=No to Run=Yes[This enables saned to run automatically].

- Make sure Run_As_User=saned is present and not commented out.

- Save changes and exit.

Edit saned.conf with **sudo nano /etc/sane.d/saned.conf**

- Add the following line to enable any device on your local network (assumes default gateway/router is at 192.168.1.1) to connect to the scanner:

    - 192.168.1.0/24

- Save changes and exit.

Next, use an **ls -l** command to determine the ownership of the 007 file used by the scanner (Figure 6-22):

sudo ls -l /dev/bus/usb/001

```
pi@raspberrypi:~ $ sudo ls -l/dev/bus/usb/001
ls: invalid option -- '/'
Try 'ls --help' for more information.
pi@raspberrypi:~ $ sudo ls -l /dev/bus/usb/001
total 0
crw-rw-r--  1 root root 189, 0 May  2 17:23 001
crw-rw-r--  1 root root 189, 1 May  1 21:55 002
crw-rw-r--  1 root root 189, 2 May  2 17:23 003
crw-rw-r--  1 root root 189, 3 May  2 17:23 004
crw-rw-r--  1 root root 189, 4 May  2 17:23 005
crw-rw-r--  1 root root 189, 5 May  2 17:23 006
crw-rw-r--+ 1 root lp   189, 6 May  2 17:58 007
pi@raspberrypi:~ $
```

Figure 6-22. *Determining the ownership of the 007 file used by the HP OfficeJet multifunction device*

The output shows that 007 is owned by the lp group. To add a user to that group, use the adduser command:

sudo adduser saned lp

[or **sudo usermod -a -G lp saned**]
To enable and restart the saned.socket unit, use these commands:

sudo systemctl enable saned.socket
sudo systemctl restart saned.socket

Reboot the system with sudo reboot after making these changes.

Connecting to SANE from Windows

There are several scanner apps available for Windows that support SANE scanners on a network:

- SaneTWAIN http://sanetwain.ozuzo.net/

- SANEWinDS https://sourceforge.net/projects/sanewinds/

- xSANE Win32 www.npackd.org/p/org.xsane.xsane/0.991

- SwingSANE http://swingsane.com/

SaneTWAIN was designed for 32-bit versions of Windows, but will run in 64-bit versions of Windows. To get it to run, use the following compatibility settings: Windows XP Service Pack 2, Run as Administrator.

SANEWinDS supports a wide variety of output file types, but it does not offer a preview mode for selecting photo size dynamically. If you don't like the original scan, you must perform an additional scan after making changes.

xSANE Win32 has not been updated for several years, and works with scanners that are supported by standard SANE backends. It does not support scanners or all-in-one units that rely on additional software, such as HP.

SwingSANE uses JAVA to connect to SANE backends on other devices. It does not require scanner drivers to be configured on the client PC.

Connecting to SANE from MacOS (OSX)

MacOS supports SANE scanners hosted on Raspberry Pi or other Linux devices using third-party SANE-TWAIN for MacOS X (`www.ellert.se/twain-sane/`; see `https://macmanus.nl/2015/11/10/fixed-use-unsupported-scanner-in-osx-10-11-el_capitan/` for installation order and other help). SwingSANE can also be used with OSX (MacOS).

Unfortunately, Linux-hosted all-in-one devices are detected by Printer and Scanner preferences as printers because of the CUPS driver used to share the device.

SANE's standard list of scanners is very outdated. If MacOS were a true Linux distro, you could install Linux multifunction drivers available from HP (HPLIP), Epson, and so on. Unfortunately, MacOS is not Linux, although it uses a Linux-like terminal interface that supports many Linux commands.

If you need access to the scanner on an all-in-one (multifunction) device on a network that includes Linux, Windows, and MacOS (OSX) devices, consider using a MacOS or Windows computer as the host.

Headless Boot

If you plan to use your Raspberry Pi as a dedicated print/scan server, you want it to be as inconspicuous as possible. Ditching the display, mouse, and keyboard and using SSH for remote access and headless booting enables you to put the Pi anywhere it can be powered. You can use raspi-config to set up your Raspberry Pi:

1. **sudo raspi-config**

2. Select **Advanced options**

3. Select **SSH**

4. Enabled? **<Yes>**

5. **<OK>**

6. **<Finish>**

Connecting via SSH Using Windows

To connect with your Raspberry Pi via SSH, you can use browser-based extensions such as FireSSH (Firefox), Secure Shell for Chrome, a Windows GUI such as PuTTY, or a command-line app (Cygwin). PuTTY is the most often-recommended Windows utility, and it is the app we use in this chapter.

Note   To learn more about using SSH in Windows, see www.makeuseof.com/tag/4-easy-ways-to-use-ssh-in-windows/.

PuTTY is available from www.chiark.greenend.org.uk/~sgtatham/putty/latest.html. It's available in 32-bit or 64-bit Windows versions as well as a UNIX archive. If you prefer to choose the components you like, the SSH and Telnet, SCP, SFTP, and other PuTTY components can also be downloaded separately.

To connect to a remote computer (such as your Raspberry Pi) using PuTTY:

1. Start PuTTY

2. Enter the IP address for the remote computer

3. Make sure SSH is selected as the connection type

4. Click **Open** (Figure 6-23)

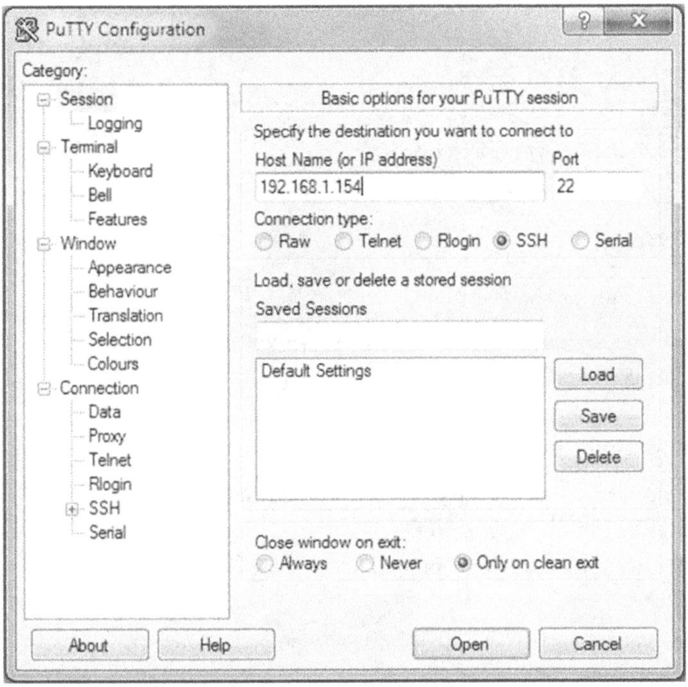

Figure 6-23. *Preparing to log into a Raspberry Pi with PuTTY*

After making the connection, enter the username and password you use for the Raspberry Pi (Figure 6-24).

```
pi@raspberrypi: ~
login as: pi
pi@192.168.1.154's password:
Access denied
pi@192.168.1.154's password:

The programs included with the Debian GNU/Linux system are free software;
the exact distribution terms for each program are described in the
individual files in /usr/share/doc/*/copyright.

Debian GNU/Linux comes with ABSOLUTELY NO WARRANTY, to the extent
permitted by applicable law.
Last login: Thu Apr 20 18:07:31 2017
pi@raspberrypi:~ $
```

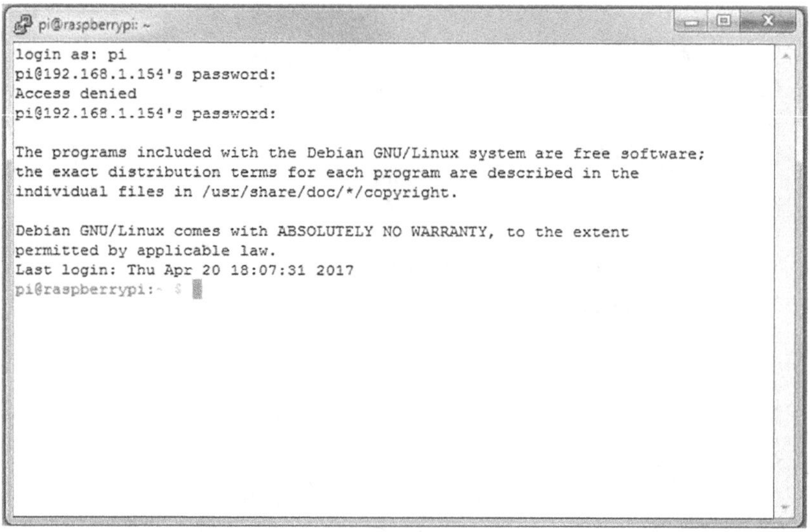

Figure 6-24. Logging into the Raspberry Pi via SSH

Troubleshooting

If you cannot connect to a printer share remotely:

- Make sure the Raspberry Pi has a working network connection with ifconfig
- Make sure the Raspberry Pi is in the same workgroup as the computer you are connecting from
- Make sure you have entered the correct IP address and port number to open CUPS on the Raspberry Pi
- Make sure CUPS has been configured to permit network connections
- Make sure Samba has been installed and is properly configured
- Make sure you have installed the correct drivers on your client system

If you cannot find a printer driver you can use with CUPS:

- Make sure you have installed the correct drivers for use by CUPS

- If you have drivers for similar models, try a similar model's driver, perform a test print, and see if it works

If you cannot find a scanner driver you can use with SANE:

- Make sure you have installed the correct drivers for use by SANE

- If you have drivers for similar models, try a similar model's driver, perform a test scan, and see if it works

If you cannot connect to SANE remotely:

- Make sure you have installed the drivers needed to connect to SANE on your computer (varies by SANE helper app)

Summary

Almost all printers, scanners, and multifunction devices connect via USB ports. You might need to add a USB hub to your Raspberry Pi if it doesn't have an available USB port. Following are additional tasks covered:

- Use a GUI-less (command-line) distro such as Raspbian Jessie Lite and install it to a hard disk.

- You might need to manually configure your Raspberry Pi to use a wireless connection.

- Use CUPS to configure your printer or multifunction device's print features.

- If CUPS does not have built-in support for your printer or multifunction device, search for and install a suitable printer driver.

- Use Samba to enable your Raspberry Pi to receive print and scan jobs.

- To connect to your printer with Windows, use View Devices and Printers (Windows 7) or Settings (Windows 8.1/10).

- To connect to your printer with MacOS (OSX), use Printer and Scanners from System Preferences.

- Use SANE to configure your scanner or multifunction device's scanner features.

- You can choose from a variety of Windows and MacOS (OSX) scanner apps to access a scanner controlled by SANE.

- Enable SSH if you want to boot your Raspberry Pi without a keyboard or display.

## CHAPTER 7

Imaging and Video

Thanks to its onboard USB port(s) and camera connector, a Raspberry Pi can be a small, yet powerful imaging and video tool. In this chapter, you learn how to use the camera connector to connect to cameras made especially for the Pi, connect to webcams made for PCs, capture stills and video from these sources, and scan images and documents with a multifunction device or dedicated image scanner.

Hardware Used in This Chapter

- Raspberry Pi (various models)

- Raspberry Pi camera

- Webcam

- Image scanners

Connecting a Camera to the Camera Port

Almost all Raspberry Pi models (with the exception of the earliest Pi Zero) feature a camera port. Cameras made for the Raspberry Pi (Figure 7-1) are available in two types:

- 5-megapixel (5MP) resolution (shown)

- 8MP resolution

© Mark Edward Soper 2017

M. E. Soper, *Expanding Your Raspberry Pi*, DOI 10.1007/978-1-4842-2922-4_7

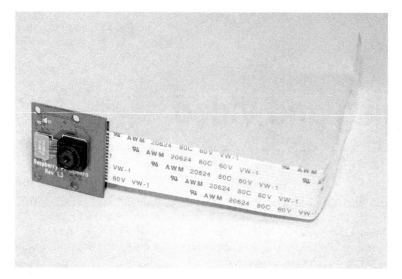

Figure 7-1. *The 5MP version of the Raspberry Pi camera with the normal interface cable attached*

■ **Note**   The 5MP version is labeled Raspberry Pi Camera Rev 1.3 and uses a green printed circuit board (PCB), as shown in Figure 7-1. The 8MP version is labeled Raspberry Pi Camera v2.3 and has a green PCB. The NoIR versions designed for near-infrared imaging have black PCBs. For technical details, see http://elinux.org/Rpi_Camera_Module.

Both versions include a detachable ribbon cable that connects to the camera port. Pi Zero models with a camera port use a smaller cable (available separately) to connect to the camera port on the end of the board (refer to Figure 7-3).

Follow this procedure to safely connect the camera cable to the camera port on all models other than the Raspberry Pi Zero:

1. Shut down the Raspberry Pi (**sudo shutdown**)

2. Disconnect power to the Raspberry Pi

3. Discharge any static electricity in your body by touching a metal object

4. Remove the camera from its antistatic bag

5. Pull up the two side clips on the camera port; use tweezers to help perform this task if the Pi is in a case

6. Slide the cable into the camera port, making sure the silver-colored connectors are facing toward the HDMI port (Figure 7-2)

Figure 7-2. Inserting the camera cable into the Raspberry Pi camera port (left) and securing the cable clamp (right)

7. Push down on the side clips to hold the cable in place

8. After checking your installation, connect power to the Raspberry Pi and boot it

Swapping Cables for a Raspberry Pi Zero

The original version of the Raspberry Pi Zero did not include a camera port. However, starting with version 1.3, and with all versions of the Raspberry Pi Zero W (which includes Wi-Fi and Bluetooth support), you can connect a Raspberry Pi camera to the Pi Zero. However, a cable swap is needed, as the Pi Zero camera port is significantly smaller than the camera port used by other Pi modules:

1. Pull up the two side clips on the camera's cable connector

2. Slide the cable out of the camera

3. Connect the Raspberry Pi Zero camera cable into the camera, making sure the connectors are facing toward the camera's PCB (Figure 7-3)

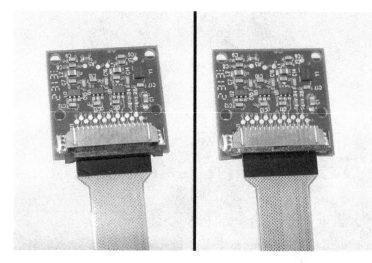

Figure 7-3. *Sliding the Pi Zero camera cable into the camera connector (left) and snapping the clamp shut (right)*

4. Push down on the side clips to hold the cable in place

5. Pull up the two side clips on the Pi Zero's camera cable connector

6. Slide the narrow end of the cable into the camera cable connector, making sure the connector side is facing the Pi Zero PCB (Figure 7-4)

Figure 7-4. *Sliding the Pi Zero camera cable into the Pi Zero/Zero W camera connector (top) and snapping the clamp shut (bottom)*

7. Snap the retaining clamp shut

8. After checking your installation, connect power to the Raspberry Pi Zero or Zero W and boot it

Enabling the Camera Port

The camera port is not enabled in the default Raspbian Lite installation. To enable it, follow these steps:

1. **`sudo raspi-config`**

2. Select **5. Interfacing options**

3. Select **P1. Camera** (Figure 7-5)

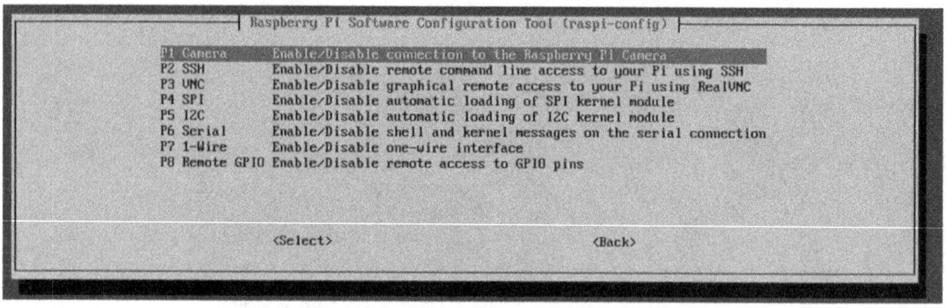

Figure 7-5. Enabling the Raspberry Pi camera using `raspi-config`

4. Press the **Enter** key twice to enable the camera option

5. Select **Finish**

6. Restart your Raspberry Pi (**sudo restart**) and the camera will be available for use after you log in

---

■ **Note** If you use Ubuntu MATE instead of Raspbian, you can still use raspi-config to configure your Raspberry Pi. See `https://larrylisky.com/2016/11/24/enabling-raspberry-pi-camera-v2-under-ubuntu-mate/` for details.

If you are unable to use raspi-config to enable your Raspberry Pi camera, edit your Pi's config.txt file thus:

1. **sudo nano /boot/config.txt** [using the default nano editor]

2. start_x=1 [x=0 disables the camera]

3. gpu_mem=125 [minimum system RAM to use for Pi's GPU; use 160 (megabytes) with a 1GB or larger RPi]

4. Save changes with Ctrl-X, Y, and Enter, and exit editor

5. **sudo reboot**

■ **Tip** The BerryBoot boot manager might prevent raspi-config from running in its default installation. To fix this problem, see `https://raspberrypi.stackexchange.com/questions/50642/sudo-raspi-config-not-working-boot-partition-not-mounted`.

The camera port is enabled in the default Raspbian with PIXEL (PIXEL is the default GUI in a Raspbian Jessie installation). To verify that it is enabled:

1. Click the Raspberry icon in the upper left-hand corner to open the RPi menu

2. Click **Preferences**

3. Click **Raspberry Pi Configuration**

4. Click the **Interfaces** tab

5. If Camera is set as Disabled, click **Enabled** (see Figure 7-6)

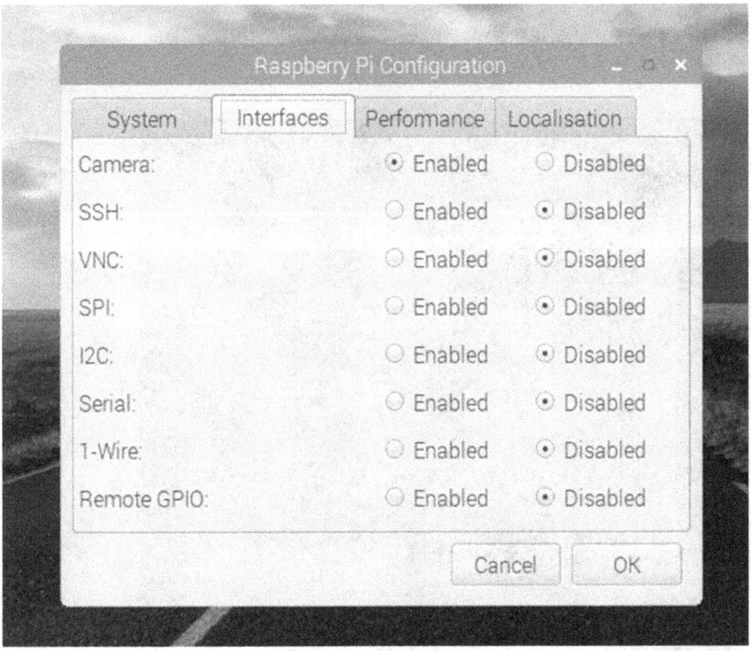

Figure 7-6. *Enabling the Raspberry Pi camera using Raspbian with PIXEL*

6. Click **OK**

Using Raspivid to Capture Video

Both Raspbian and Raspbian Lite include the command-line raspivid video capture utility. Raspivid can be run from any user account; it does not require root access. It has many options for resolution, preview size, image effects, metering, and many others.

Raspivid Options and Examples

To see all of the options supported by raspivid, enter **raspivid |more**. For more details, see http://elinux.org/Rpi_Camera_Module#RaspiVid. Here are a few examples [explanations in square brackets]:

- `-d` [Runs raspivid in demonstration mode, using the various metering, color, and other special modes]

- `-t 0` [sets raspivid to run until the program is canceled with Ctrl-C; no image will be saved. When the -t option is not used, recording runs for 5000ms/5 seconds]

- `-t 15000` [captures video for 15000ms/5 seconds]

- `-ifx negative` [reverses colors as in a color negative; see Figure 7-7]

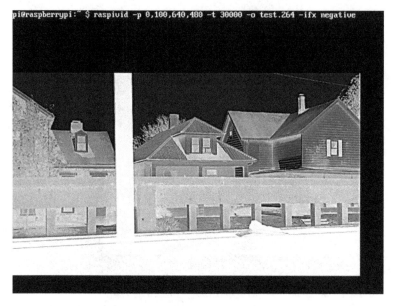

Figure 7-7. Running raspivid from the command prompt in Raspbian Jessie Lite

- `-ifx cartoon` [makes video appear as it's in a cartoon]

- `-ifx gpen` [black and white, no gray scale, pen effect; see Figure 7-8]

Figure 7-8. Running raspivid from a terminal session in Raspbian Jessie with PIXEL

- -awb incandescent [sets white balance for incandescent light (about 2700-3200K)]

- -mm backlit [sets metering mode for backlit scenes]

- -fps 30 [sets framerate to 30fps]

- -w 1280 [sets recording width to 1280 pixels]

- -h 720 [sets recording height to 720 pixels]

- -o test.264 [saves recording as test.264; use any file name desired]

- -hf [flip image horizontally]

In the example shown in Figure 7-7, raspivid is run from the command prompt on a system using Raspbian Jessie Lite. When a preview window is used, it overlays any text already onscreen.

raspivid -p 0,100,640,480 -t 30000 -o test.264 -ifx negative

In the example shown in Figure 7-8, raspivid is run from the command prompt after opening a terminal session with Raspbian Jessie with Pixel. When a preview window is used, it is displayed in a separate window.

raspivid -p 1,1,640,480 -ifx gpen -t 0

Playing Videos with OMXplayer

To play back your videos with Raspbian Lite, install the OMXPlayer program:

```
sudo apt-get update
sudo apt-get omxplayer
```

To play a video called test.264 with omxplayer's normal settings:

```
omxplayer test.264
```

By default, omxplayer plays videos in full-screen, stretching the image if necessary. To see all options for omxplayer, enter omxplayer |more

Here are two examples [explanations in square brackets}:

- -l 00:02:37 [start video at 2 minute-37 second mark]

- -aspect-mode letterbox [plays video without stretching to fill screen]

Converting Recordings with MP4Box

By default raspivid captures videos as raw H.264 streams. However, most video players cannot play back H.264 or other raw video streams unless they are packaged as a common video format, such as MP4.

■ **Note** When I saved video files using the .264 extension and copied them to a Windows computer, Windows Media Player displayed a warning that the file type was unknown, but it played the files. However, Apple Quick Time could not play the files at all.

The MP4Box utility provides a simple command-line method for file conversion. MP4Box is contained in the GPAC Project on Advanced Content. To install it on your Raspberry Pi:

```
sudo apt-get update
```

> **sudo apt-get install gpac** [if prompted after using this command, rerun this command with --fix-missing]

MP4Box (note the capitalization) has many options. To see them, run

```
MP4Box
```

To convert a file called test.264 into an MP4 file called test.mp4 running at 30fps, use this command:

```
MP4Box -fps 30 -add test.264 test.mp4
```

The mp4 file played flawlessly on Windows Media Player. MP4Box can only convert one file at a time. However, by using a Python script (see http://raspi.tv/2013/ another-way-to-convert-raspberry-pi-camera-h264-output-to-mp4 for details), you can convert multiple files from the command line.

Note To learn more about gpac or to download versions for other platforms, see https://packages.debian.org/jessie/gpac.

Using Raspistill to Take Photos

The raspistill program, like raspivid, is included in Raspbian and Raspbian Lite. Raspistill, like Raspivid, can be run from any user account; it does not require root access. It has many options for resolution, preview size, image effects, metering, and many others.

Raspistill's commands and syntax are similar to those in Raspivid. To see all of the commands, enter **raspistill |more**. For more details, see http://elinux.org/Rpi_ Camera_Module#RaspiStill. Here are some examples:

- -sh -100 [minimum sharpness; maximum is 100]
- -ifx sketch [sharp edges are outlined, colors are faded]
- -ifx film [simulated film grain]
- -w 2048 [sets photo width to 2048 pixels]
- -h 1536 [sets photo height to 1536 pixels]
- -o image.jpg [saves photo as image.jpg]
- -hf [flip image horizontally]

Figure 7-9 illustrates the use of -ifx sketch.

Figure 7-9. A demonstration of the -ifx sketch special effects setting with raspistill

Taking Time-Lapse Photos with Raspistill

Raspistill includes options that can be used to take time-lapse sequences:

- -tl [timelapse; -tl 60000 takes a picture every 60000ms/60 seconds]
- -t [total time to capture photos; -t 3600000 takes pictures at the interval set by -tl for 3,600,000ms/60 minutes]
- -o photo_%04d.jpg [captures image as photo_0001.jpg, etc.]

The following command displays a 640×480 preview at 100 pixels from the left and 100 pixels from the top of the display, sets sharpness at the maximum level, adjusts EV 12 (values are –25 to 25, each step is 1/6 stop), uses a shutter speed of .2 or 1/5 second, takes a picture every 60 seconds for one hour, saving each picture as photo_xxxx.jpg (starting with 0001):

```
raspistill -p 100,100,640,480 -sh 100 -ev 12 -ss 20000 -tl 60000 -t3600000
-o photo_%04d.jpg
```

■ **Tip**   By default, the red LED activity light on the camera module blinks when you take a picture or shoot a video. This could affect the quality of time-lapse photos or videos shot in dim light or startle some subjects. To disable this option, edit the /boot/config.txt file and make the following change: `disable_camera_led=1` Save your changes, restart your Raspberry Pi, and your camera will no longer blink while shooting. To re-enable the LED, edit /boot/config.txt and change the line to `disable_camera_led=0`.

Viewing Raspistill Photo Metadata

Raspistill, like almost any other camera app, stores exposure and other information in the picture file itself. This metadata (also known as EXIF data) can be viewed in any recent version of Windows by following these steps (steps in parentheses are for touchscreens):

1. Right-click (press and hold) the picture file in Windows Explorer/File Explorer

2. Click (tap) **Properties**

3. Click (tap) the **Details** tab

4. Scroll down to the **Image** and **Camera** sections for resolution, f-stop, shutter speed, exposure time, and other settings [see Figure 7-10]

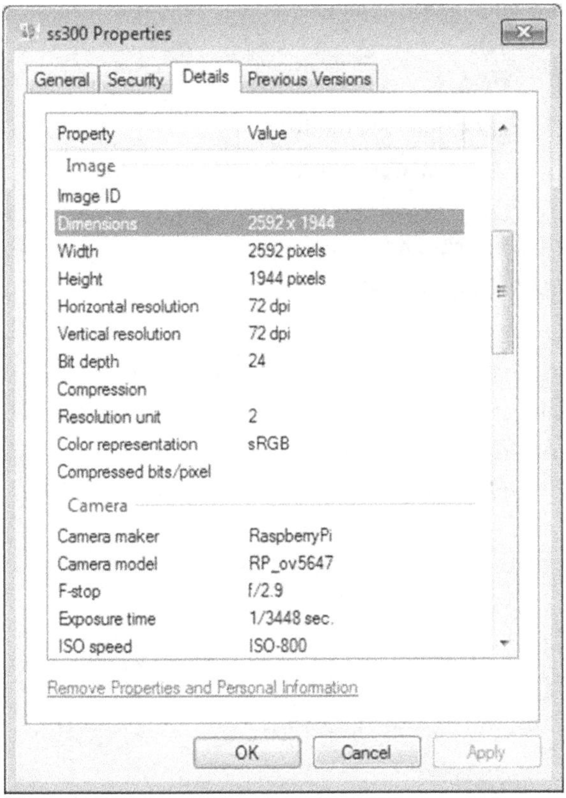

Figure 7-10. *Viewing exposure and camera metadata with Windows Explorer*

5. Click (tap) **OK** to close the Properties dialog

> ■ **Tip** To view EXIF data on a system running MacOS (OSX), open the Photos app, point to a picture, and Control-click it. From the menu, select **Get Info**. In addition to seeing camera, lens, and exposure data, you can also add a title, description, keyword, and location.

Controlling the Raspberry Pi Camera with Python

The Python 3.x programming language is already installed in Raspian Jessie with PIXEL. To install picamera, the Python package for using the Raspberry Pi camera module, use the following commands:

```
sudo easy_install3 picamera
```

Immediately afterward, use this command to update to the latest version of picamera:

```
sudo easy_install3 -U picamera
```

Picamera has two advantages over raspistills and raspivid:

- You can create scripts ("recipes") that you can store and reuse.

- Picamera provides many more options for controlling capture settings and output than Raspistill and Raspivid.

To use picamera, open a Python session from the command line: python

> ■ **Tip** When you use picamera in a Python script, the camera preview covers up most or all of your screen. Use SSH to log into your Pi from another system and run Python remotely (Figure 7-11). The remote session will enable you to start Python and enter or paste in script commands because the camera preview window is displayed on the Raspberry Pi's own display.

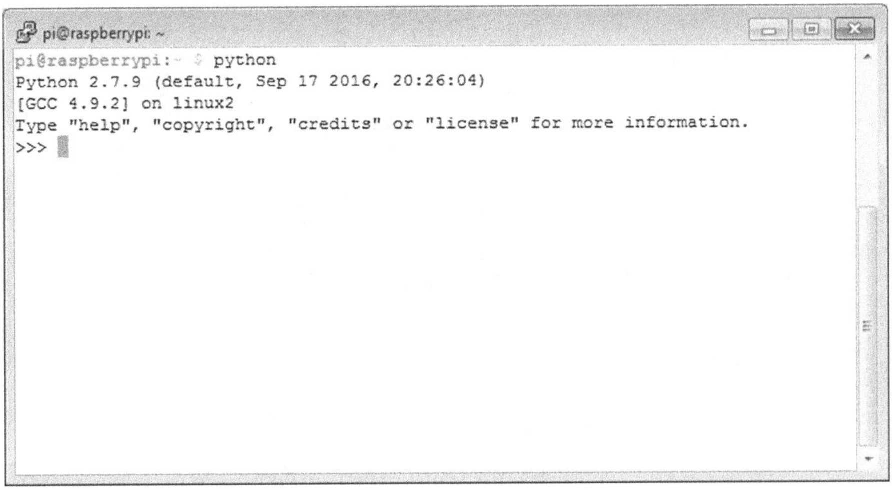

Figure 7-11. *Starting Python remotely using SSH. Enter Python commands or paste in a script at the >>> prompt.*

For complete coverage of picamera, go to https://picamera.readthedocs.io/en/release-1.13/. Here is a script adapted from this source. This version captures a 3.1MP photo:

```
from time import sleep
from picamera import PiCamera

camera = PiCamera()
camera.resolution = (2048,1536)
camera.start_preview()
# Camera warm-up time
sleep(2)
camera.capture('test.jpg')
```

Here is another script adapted from this source. This version captures two H.264 video streams at the same time in two different resolutions (Figure 7-12):

```
import picamera

with picamera.PiCamera() as camera:
    camera.resolution = (1280, 1024)
    camera.framerate = 30
    camera.start_recording('highres.h264')
    camera.start_recording('lowres.h264', splitter_port=2, resize=(640, 480))
    camera.wait_recording(30)
    camera.stop_recording(splitter_port=2)
    camera.stop_recording()
```

137

```
pi@raspberrypi: ~
pi@raspberrypi:~ $ python
Python 2.7.9 (default, Sep 17 2016, 20:26:04)
[GCC 4.9.2] on linux2
Type "help", "copyright", "credits" or "license" for more information.
>>> import picamera
>>>
>>> with picamera.PiCamera() as camera:
...     camera.resolution = (1280, 1024)
...     camera.framerate = 30
...     camera.start_recording('highres.h264')
...     camera.start_recording('lowres.h264', splitter_port=2, resize=(640, 480)
)
...     camera.wait_recording(30)
...     camera.stop_recording(splitter_port=2)
...     camera.stop_recording()
...
>>> exit
Use exit() or Ctrl-D (i.e. EOF) to exit
>>> exit ()
pi@raspberrypi:~ $
```

Figure 7-12. *Using picamera in a Python script to create two video files with different resolutions at the same time. Use* exit *( ) to close Python.*

Controlling Your Raspberry Pi Camera with Android or iOS

Whether you use an Android smartphone or tablet or an iOS iPhone or iPad, you can use your Raspberry Pi camera remotely and enjoy the benefits of easy control of the Pi camera's many options.

Using RaspiCAM Remote for Android

There are a number of Raspberry Pi camera apps available in Google Play (the Android app store). RaspiCAM Remote is a free app with high ratings, minimal setup requirements, and video or still photo capture, so we chose it as the example Android app for this book.

When you open RaspiCAM Remote, the startup dialog prompts you to enter the IP address and login information for the Raspberry Pi (Figure 7-13). Click the connect (double-cable plug) icon to connect to your Raspberry Pi.

Figure 7-13. *Using RaspiCAM Remote to connect to a Raspberry Pi*

After you connect, use the icons at the bottom of the screen to open the setup menu, select video mode (enabled in this example), select still photo mode, or capture a video/image (Figure 7-14). RaspiCAM Remote provides a live preview of what the camera sees with the effects and settings you select, making it easy to capture the video or photo you want.

Figure 7-14. *RaspiCAM's shooting menu (center), setup menu (left), and image settings menu (right). Tap the floppy disc icon to shoot video or grab a still photo.*

RaspiCAM Remote's pictures are stored on your Android device, rather than on your Raspberry Pi, so you don't need to copy them manually between your computer and your Android device. In Gallery, look for them in the Pictures section.

Using BerryCam for iOS

BerryCam, which captures still images only, requires the user to install the berryCam.py Python script on the Raspberry Pi as well as install a client app on the mobile device. This script is required to enable BerryCam clients to connect to the Raspberry Pi and use its camera. To install BerryCam on the Raspberry Pi, go to `http://fotosyn.com/berrycam/repo/` and follow the directions.

After berryCam is installed on the Raspberry Pi, open it using this command (Figure 7-15): **sudo python berryCam.py &**

```
pi@raspberrypi: ~
pi@raspberrypi:~ $ sudo python berryCam.py &
[1] 1136
pi@raspberrypi:~ $ B E R R Y C A M -- Listening on port 8000
Please ensure your BerryCam App is installed and running on your iOS Device
```

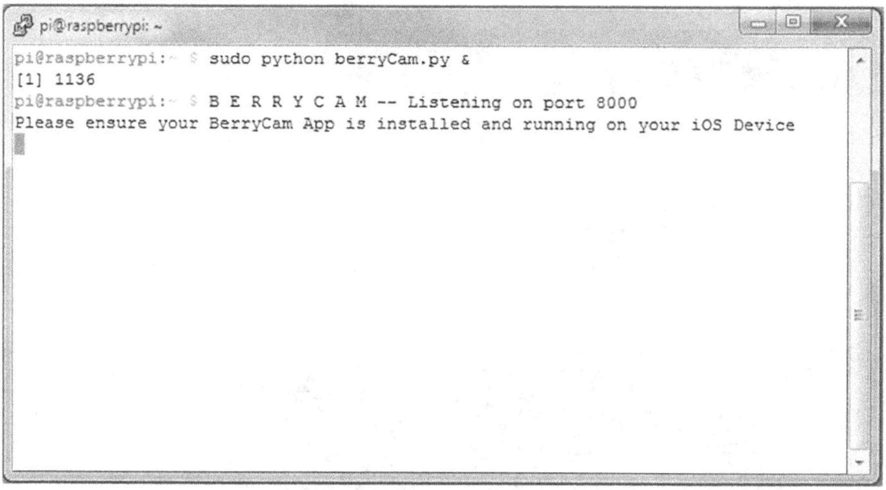

Figure 7-15. *Starting the berryCam script on the Raspberry Pi*

As long as this script is running, you can connect to your Raspberry Pi from an iOS device running the BerryCam app.

To log into the Raspberry Pi and take pictures, install the BerryCam app from the App Store. When you start it, click the settings (gearbox) icon shown on the opening dialog and enter the correct IP address for your Raspberry Pi (Figure 7-16). Make any other adjustments you want, then tap Done (top left of the Settings dialog).

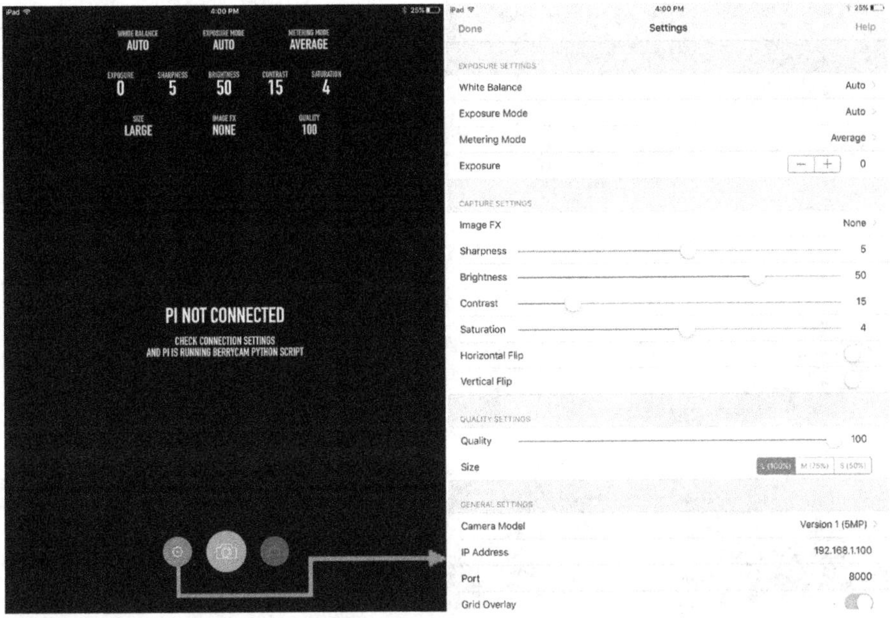

Figure 7-16. *When you start the BerryCam client in iOS (left), you must enter the correct IP address for the Raspberry Pi on the Settings screen (right)*

To capture an image with BerryCam, press the camera button. After the capture is made, it is displayed on your iOS device along with the camera settings (Figure 7-17). Use the initial capture to point the camera in the right direction and to make changes in camera settings.

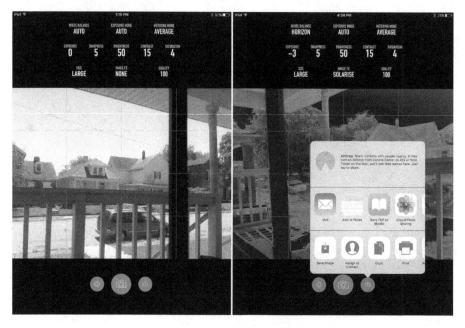

Figure 7-17. *Capturing an image with default settings (left) and with custom exposure, white balance, and special effects settings (right)*

By default, images captured by BerryCam are stored in the berrycam folder on your Raspberry Pi. The captures for each date are stored in a folder named after the capture date.

When you capture an image, click the upload button shown in Figure 7-17 to have the option to save your images to your iOS device. If you choose this option, the pictures will not be stored on your Raspberry Pi.

■ **Note** The first time you choose to save images to your iOS from BerryCam, you are prompted to give permission to the BerryCam app. If you don't give permission to the app, the pictures will be stored on the Raspberry Pi.

For users who want to connect from an iOS, Android, Windows, Windows Mobile, Linux, or MacOS (OSX) device to a Raspberry Pi camera using the same BerryCam interface, you can download BerryCam Express from https://pitography.github.io/BerryCamExpress/. BerryCam Express provides source code so that user can also learn modern programming techniques.

Using a Webcam with a Raspberry Pi

There are several ways to use a USB webcam with a Raspberry Pi:

- Install a simple command-line webcam package such as fswebcam

- Install a GUI-based webcam package such as guvcview

- Use the USB option available in RaspiCAM Remote

Using Fswebcam

To install the fswebcam package:

```
sudo apt-get install fswebcam
```

To capture an image called webcampic.jpg using the default resolution:

```
fswebcam webcampic.jpg
```

During the capture, your system displays the resolution used to capture the image (see Figure 7-18). As you can see, the default resolution is extremely low, matching the resolution of the very first USB webcams available over a decade ago. Fswebcam does not provide a preview image. To aim the webcam as desired, open the first image capture you make and use it to help aim the webcam. In Figure 7-18, we used the file manager in Raspbian with PIXEL to display the captured image. Note that the default image has an image capture time banner along the bottom edge.

Figure 7-18. Fswebcam used with default settings (left) captures a small image from a webcam (right)

To get a higher-quality image, specify the webcam's recommended resolution with the -r option. To omit the banner, use the --no-banner option (Figure 7-19):

```
fswebcam -r 1920x1080 --no-banner webcampic_HD.jpg
```

Figure 7-19. *Specifying the resolution and no-banner options produces a larger, higher-quality image with no distracting banner on the bottom edge of the image*

■ **Note** To learn more about using a webcam with Raspberry Pi, see www.raspberrypi. org/documentation/usage/webcams/. If you are wanting to purchase a webcam for use with Raspberry Pi, see http://elinux.org/RPi_USB_Webcams for test results. The webcam used in this section was a Logitech HD Pro Webcam C910 with autofocus.

Capturing Video or Stills Using Guvcview

If you want to use a single package to capture video or still images from a USB webcam, install the guvcview package:

sudo apt-get guvcview

If you install this using Add / Remove Software in Raspbian with PIXEL GUI, this package is listed as GTK+ base UVC Viewer.

Guvcview is designed to work with many image and audio sources and to output image and video files. It has many options. To see them, enter

guvcview --help-all

The following command line starts guvcview without audio [-ao none], with YUYV image format enabled [-f YUYV], a resolution of 640×480 [-x 640x480], and video capture (if selected) using H264 [-u h264]:

```
guvcview -ao none -f YUYV -x 640x480 -u h264
```

When guvcview starts, it opens a preview window, a control panel window, and display status information in the original command-line window (Figure 7-20). The control panel provides separate settings for image controls, H264 format controls, video controls, and audio controls. You can also select the video/still and audio inputs to use if more than one are available.

Figure 7-20. *While guvcview runs, you can use the control panel (right) to adjust exposure, video, and audio settings and capture video or still images. The preview window (center) shows volume settings when recording video, and a steady stream of status messages are displayed in the terminal window (left).*

Using RaspiCAM Remote with a Webcam

RaspiCAM Remote also works with USB webcams. To use it with a webcam:

1. Start RaspiCAM Remote

2. Open the setup menu (refer to Figure 7-14).

3. Select USB.

4. Close the app.

5. Restart it.

6. Select the capture option (video or stills).

Figure 7-21 shows the author's smartphone controlling the webcam on his Raspberry Pi.

Figure 7-21. *RaspiCAM Remote capturing a still image while being controlled by the author's Samsung Galaxy 6 smartphone*

Connecting to an Image Scanner

Raspbian with PIXEL also supports many image scanner packages, once you install SANE (Scanner Access Now Easy). In Chapter 6, we discuss how to use SANE for scanning remotely. In this chapter, we discuss how to install SANE and packages that enable you to scan, adjust, and save images directly on your Raspberry Pi.

Installing SANE with PIXEL, Other Linux GUIs

SANE, the backends, and the frontends needed can all be downloaded from the Raspbian with PIXEL software repository. In this example, I will be installing scanning components needed to use the scanner built into the Epson XP-800 multifunction device.

After searching for SANE in the software repository (Add / Remove Software), I selected the following packages (version numbers omitted, as these change over time):

- Xsane

- Xsane-common

- Sane scanner graphical frontends (sane)

- Simple scanning utility (simple-scan)

- API library for scanners (libsane)

- API library for scanners: extra backends(libsane)

- API library for scanners: utilities (sane-utils)

Click Apply to start the process. After providing your password and clicking OK, the installation process continues. During the installation process, SANE checks for local or network scanners and identifies them. To determine if a scanner (or scanner component of a multifunction device) is supported, go to `www.sane-project.org/sane-mfgs.html` and look up the manufacturer and model number of your scanner/multifunction device.

■ **Caution**   Epson and HP multifunction devices are well-supported by SANE in Raspbian. However, most recent Canon multifunction devices are not supported for use on Raspbian (Canon's Linux drivers are for x86 or x64 processors, not ARM processors such as those used by Raspberry Pi).

After installing SANE, try one or more of the scanning apps installed. In this chapter, we show you how to use Simple Scan and Xscan. In Raspbian with PIXEL, both can be started from the Graphics section of the Raspbian menu (Figure 7-22).

Figure 7-22. *Use the Graphics menu in Raspbian with PIXEL to start scanning utilities*

Using Simple Scan

Simple Scan supports auto document feeders (ADF). It offers simple document and photo scanning, and is a good choice for properly exposed documents and photos. To configure Simple Scan:

1. Click the scanner icon.

2. Click Preferences (Figure 7-23).

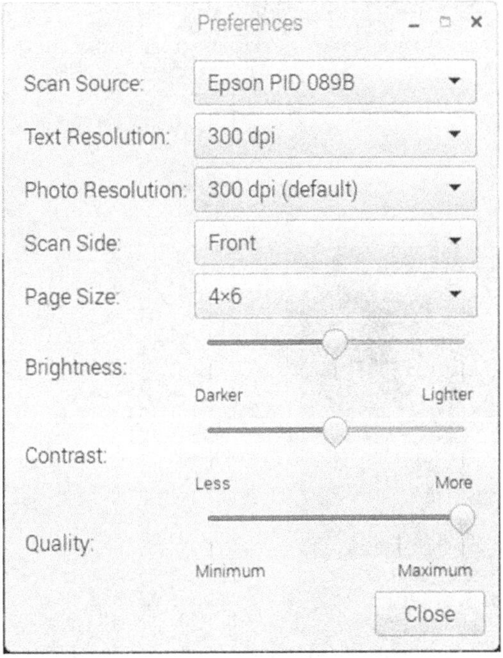

Figure 7-23. *Use the Preferences menu to adjust scan resolution, image type, scan document size, and other options*

3. If more than one scanner is available, open Scan Source to choose a different scanner.

4. Default Text resolution is 150 dpi. Open Text Resolution to change it.

5. Default Photo resolution is 300 dpi. Open Photo Resolution to change it.

6. To use an ADF, select Front and Back from the Scan Side menu.

7. To choose a specific page size, open the Page Size menu and select the size desired. If you choose 4×6, be sure to position the photo vertically against the top corner marking on the scanner.

8. Adjust Brightness, Contrast, and Quality sliders as desired.

9. Click Close when ready to scan.

To select what to scan:

1. Open the Scan menu.

2. Select All pages from feeder to use the ADF; to scan a single page from the ADF or flatbed, choose Single Page.

3. Select Text or Photo.

To scan the document or picture:

1. Click Scan (Figure 7-24).

Figure 7-24. *Rotating and cropping an image after scanning. The Save button is the second button to the left from the Simple Scan window title.*

2. Use the Rotate tools (arrows) or Crop tool (scissors) as needed.

3. After the photo or document is scanned, click the Save icon.

To save the document or picture:

1. Enter a new name (ScannedDocument.ext is the default).

2. Select the location.

3. Select the file type.

4. Click Save.

Using Xscan

Xscan offers many more scan enhancements than Simple Scan, making it suitable for use in scanning photos that may need exposure or color compensation. To configure Xscan:

1. Enter a file name (Figure 7-25).

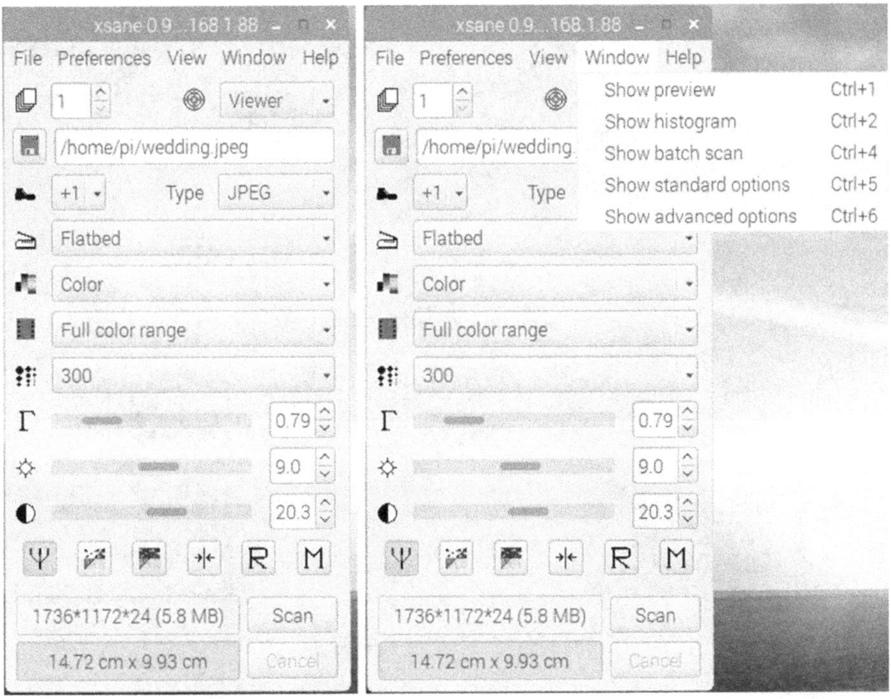

Figure 7-25. *The Xscan menu provides a full range of settings for image type and scanning options. Open the Window menu to show a scan preview or set up additional options.*

2. Select an extension.

3. Select the image source (flatbed or ADF [Auto Document Feeder]).

4. Select the image type (lineart, gray, or color).

5. If you are scanning color slides or negatives, open the Full color range menu and select the film type. Use Full color range for scanning prints.

6. To scan a photo for printing at its original size, adjust the resolution to 300. Other resolutions range from 75 to 4800.

7. Use the sliders to adjust gamma, brightness, and contrast.

8. Open the Window menu and choose Preview, Histogram, and other options as desired.

To select what to scan:

1. Open the Preview menu.

2. Click Acquire Preview (Figure 7-26).

Figure 7-26. *Preparing to scan a photo after adjusting its histogram*

3. After the preview scan is finished, adjust the size of the dotted bounding border around the area to scan.

4. To adjust the histogram in the image, open the Histogram menu and adjust the sliders along the bottom of the Raw image view.

5. To adjust the gamma, open the Gamma menu and select the desired setting.

To scan and save the document or picture:

1. Click Scan (refer to Figure 7-26).

2. Adjust the image preview size until it fits comfortably onscreen (Figure 7-27).

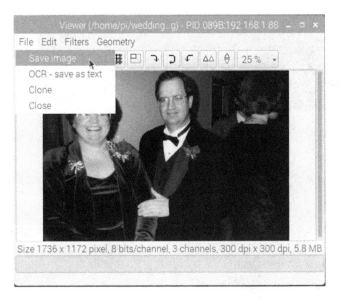

Figure 7-27. Saving the scanned photo

3. Open the File menu and click Save Image.

4. Enter a new name.

5. Select the location.

6. Select the file type.

7. Click Save.

Troubleshooting

If you have problems with the hardware or apps in this chapter, check the following:

Raspberry Pi Camera Issues

- Correct orientation of the cable when plugged into the Pi camera connector.

- If you swap cables on the camera module, be sure to check cable orientation.

- If you reversed either end of the cable and applied power, you have probably ruined your camera module.

- If you are using a 1A power supply for a Pi Zero or Pi Zero W and your system won't boot or becomes unstable, upgrade to a 2.5A or larger power supply. The camera module requires 250mA.

Camera App Issues

- You must install packages as superuser (sudo).

- If you get an error message, rerun the installation using the recommended options.

- If a package doesn't work after installation, reboot your Pi.

- If your camera app uses Python, be sure to use the recommended version.

- If you use BerryCam, the berryCam Python script must be running before you can connect from an iOS mobile device.

Network Issues

- Make sure you specify the correct IP address of your Pi when a remote app asks for it. Use ifconfig to see the Pi's IP address.

- If you switch between wired and wireless network connections, be sure to recheck the IP address.

Webcam Issues

- Shut down the Raspberry Pi before connecting a webcam. Although USB devices are supposed to be hot-swappable, it can be easy to damage your Pi if it's not in a case.

- If your Pi won't boot or becomes unstable after you connect a webcam, upgrade to a larger power supply (2.5A or higher).

- Check the webcam compatibility list if you are not sure which webcams are suitable choices.

Scanner Issues

- SANE's level of support on Raspbian and other Raspberry Pi distros lags behind versions of SANE made for x86 or x64 processor-based version of Linux such as Debian, Ubuntu, and so on.

- With an HP scanner or multifunction device, install HPlib and the HP multifunction library to enable printing and scanning.

Summary

- Cameras for the Raspberry Pi are available in 5MP and 8MP versions. Infrared (IR) versions are also available.

- To connect a camera to a Raspberry Pi Zero with a camera port or to a Pi Zero W, the standard camera cable must be swapped for a narrower replacement cable.

- Use raspi-config to enable the camera port on Raspbian Lite.

- Raspbian with PIXEL and Raspbian Lite include the command-line raspivid video capture utility.

- If you use Raspbian Lite, install the omxplayer package to play back your videos.

- Install the MP4Box package to convert H.264 video files created by raspivid into a format compatible with Apple Quick Time and other video player apps for Windows and MacOS.

- Raspbian with PIXEL and Raspbian Lite include the command-line raspistill photo capture utility.

- Raspistill can also be used to shoot time-lapse sequences.

- The picamera program for Python supports both still photo and video capture.

- To control the Raspberry Pi camera with an Android smartphone or tablet, install RaspiCAM Remote on the Android device.

- To control the Raspberry Pi camera with an iOS smartphone or tablet, install the BerryCam Python code on your Raspberry Pi and the BerryCam app on the iOS device.

- USB webcams on Raspbian/Raspbian Lite are supported by command-line (fswebcam), GUI-based (guvcview), and RaspiCAM Remote.

- To use an image scanner or the scanner function in a multifunction device, install SANE with the appropriate drivers.

- Simple Scan and Xscan are two of the many scanning apps available for Raspbian with SANE.

CHAPTER 8

Media Serving

In this chapter, you learn two ways to turn your Raspberry Pi into a media server or media playback device.

Hardware Used in This Chapter

- Raspberry Pi 3
- Wired or wireless network

Selecting a Distro

There are no shortage of media-centric Linux distros available for the Raspberry Pi. Here's a partial list, all available in BerryBoot-compatible distros from the Alex Goldscheidt BerryServer web site (`http://berryboot.alexgoldcheidt.com/`).

- LibreElec 8.0.1 (Pi 1, Zero, Zero W; Pi 2, Pi 3)
- Max2Play (Pi 2, Pi 3)
- OSMC (Pi 1, Pi Zero; Pi 2, Pi 3)
- PeachPi TV LTS (all versions)
- Pi MusicBox
- RasPlex 1.8.1 (Pi 1, Pi Zero, Pi Zero W; Pi 2, Pi 3)

In this chapter, we will examine how to set up a classic media server (LibreElec) and a Plex server client (RasPlex).

© Mark Edward Soper 2017
M. E. Soper, *Expanding Your Raspberry Pi*, DOI 10.1007/978-1-4842-2922-4_8

BerryBoot, WD PiDrive, and Media Serving

Why use BerryBoot-compatible images? BerryBoot-compatible images work very well with the WD PiDrive BerryBoot edition (1TB hard disk) and your Raspberry Pi. By using BerryBoot edition PiDrive or another 2.5-inch portable USB 3.0 hard disk drive instead of a high-capacity microSD card, you can store media on a fast, durable hard disk for faster access and relieve wear on the microSD card's flash memory.

To install any BerryBoot-compatible image, download it, extract it, copy the .IMG file to a USB flash drive, and then connect the drive to your Raspberry Pi connected to your PiDrive BerryBoot edition. Use the option to install an OS from USB flash.

■ **Note** To extract a BerryBoot .xz image file directly to an image file with Linux or MacOS (OSX), use this command from a command prompt or terminal session: `tar -Jxf name-of-the-image.img.tar.xz` (replace name-of-the-image with actual image name).

Here's the step-by-step process for Windows, starting with downloading the file to your computer. In this example, we'll use Windows along with the free 7-Zip archive file extractor. Get 7-Zip from `www.7-zip.org/`. Install it before continuing, and see the web site for the specifics of the extraction options 7-Zip offers.

1. Visit the BerryServer web site (`http://berryboot.alexgoldcheidt.com`) and select a distro by clicking the Download for Berryboot button.

2. After the file (XZ extension) is downloaded, open Windows Explorer or File Explorer, right-click the file, and select 7-Zip and one of the extraction options. The extracted file has an extension of TAR (Figure 8-1).

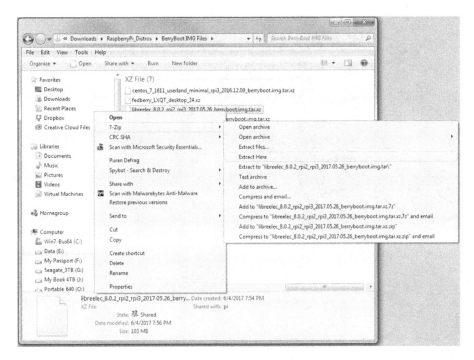

Figure 8-1. *Performing the first of two extractions with 7-Zip (XY to TAR)*

3. Right-click the .tar file, and select 7-Zip and one of the extraction options. The extracted file is the IMG file used by BerryBoot (Figure 8-2).

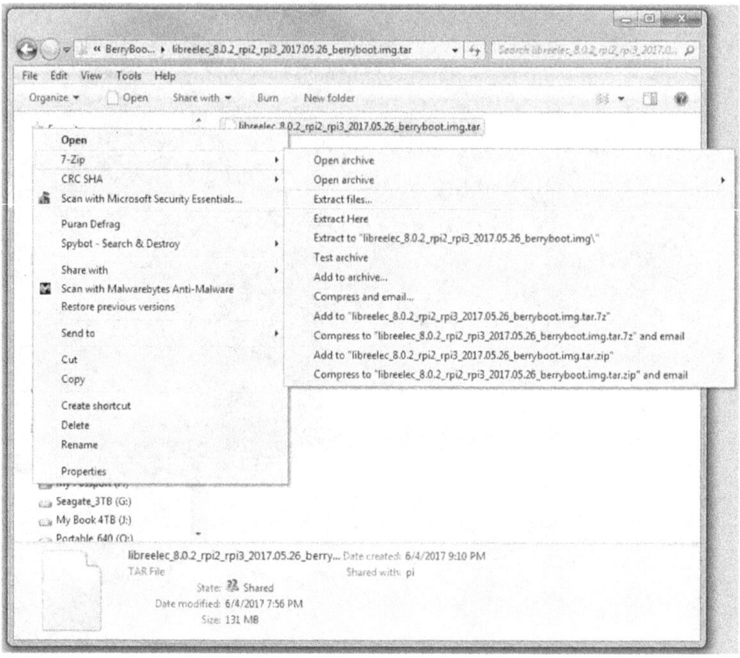

Figure 8-2. *Performing the second of two extractions with 7-Zip (TAR to IMG)*

4. Copy the IMG file to a USB flash drive that uses the default FAT32 file system.

■ **Tip** To find out what file system the flash drive uses, right-click it in Windows Explorer/ File Explorer and select Properties. The file system will be listed. If the drive is using NTFS, copy any files you want to keep, and then reformat it as FAT32. You can use the SD Formatter utility discussed in Chapter 2.

---

5. Safely eject the USB flash drive from your system.

6. Connect the USB flash drive to your Raspberry Pi running BerryBoot.

7. Start the Raspberry Pi. Select the **Edit menu** option when it appears.

8. Click the small down arrow on the Add OS button to open the menu shown in Figure 8-3.

9. Select **Copy OS from USB stick**.

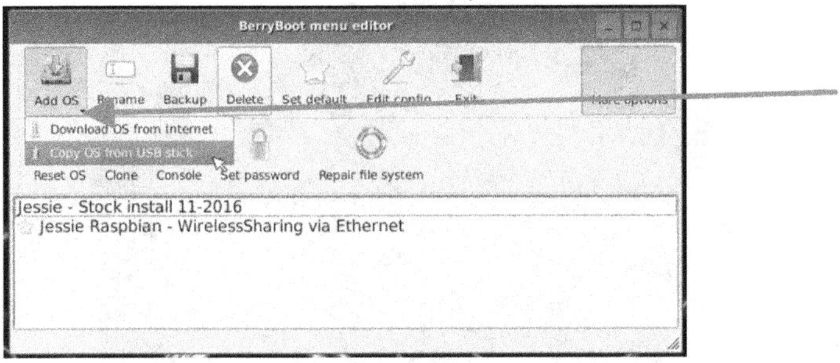

Figure 8-3. Opening the Add OS menu and selecting the Copy OS from USB stick option

10.   Select the desired .img file and click **Open**. The .img file is copied to the Raspberry Pi's drive.

11.   To make the new OS the default, select it and click **Set default** (Figure 8-4).

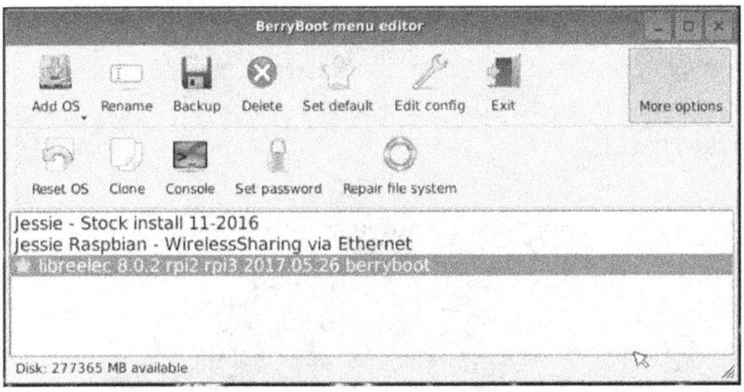

Figure 8-4. Preparing to restart the Raspberry Pi after installing LibreElec in BerryBoot

12.   Click **Exit** to restart your Raspberry Pi.

Using LibreELEC

LibreELEC is one of several Raspberry Pi distros based on the open source Kodi media player and manager. Here's how to get started.

1.   Click **Next** when prompted.

2.   The default hostname is LibreELEC. You can change it when prompted. Click **Next** after creating a new name (Figure 8-5), or to keep the existing name.

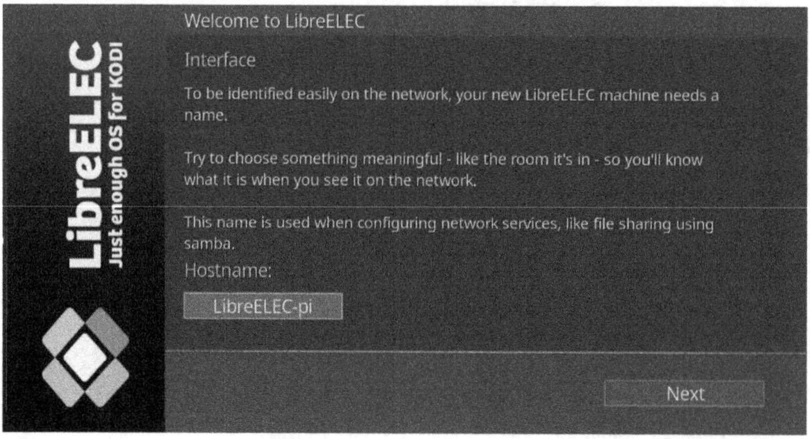

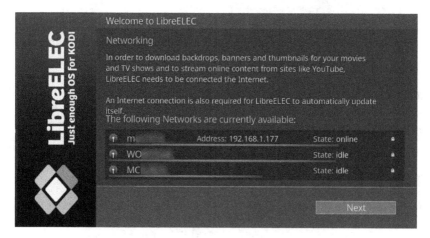

Figure 8-5. *Renaming the LibreELEC host*

3. If your Raspberry Pi is not connected to a wired network, select a wireless network from the list.

4. After you enter the password (encryption key), the network is listed as Online and your device's IP address is listed (Figure 8-6). Click Next to continue.

Figure 8-6. *Available wireless networks after connecting with one*

5. By default, Samba is enabled. You can also enable SSH. Make your choices and click **Next** to continue.

6. Click **Next** to complete setup.

Adding Media Files

LibreELEC supports playback of movies, TV shows, music, music videos, live TV radio, pictures, and videos. Whether you are using media on a local drive or a network drive, the setup process is similar.

■ **Note**   Click the Options icon (gearbox) visible in Figure 8-7 to change many different types of general and media-specific settings.

Let's look at browsing for media files on the network. We'll browse for music, but the same basic process is used for other types of media.

    1.   From the main menu (Figure 8-7), click Music.

Figure 8-7. *Beginning the process of setting up the music library*

    2.   Click **Enter files section** to browse for music.

    3.   In the Browse for library dialog, select the location that contains the files you want (Figure 8-8). Click **OK** to continue.

■ **Note**   In this example, we selected Windows network (SMB) to use files stored on a workgroup network share. Choose Network File System (NFS) to browse music files on a MacOS (OSX) computer. Scroll through the list to locate files on a local drive.

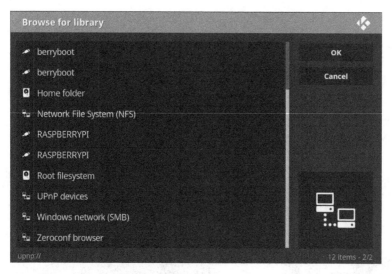

Figure 8-8. Selecting where to browse for media

4. If you select a Windows network, select the workgroup that contains the media, and click **OK**.

5. Click the network share that contains the media, and click OK.

6. If the share is password protected, you are prompted for a username and password. Provide a username and password that is already set up on that share.

7. Continue to browse until you locate the folder that includes the media you want. Click **Add** (Figure 8-9), then enter a name for the source, and click OK.

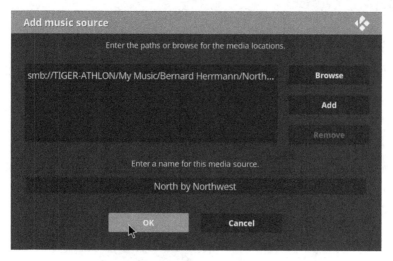

Figure 8-9. Selecting a source for music

8. Click **Yes** when prompted to add the media from the selected source to your library.

9. The source is listed the next time you open the appropriate media icon from the main menu.

10. Select the media to play.

Figure 8-10 shows a typical album listing, and Figure 8-11 shows a typical pictures folder.

Figure 8-10. *A track listing from the classic Hitchcock thriller's soundtrack album*

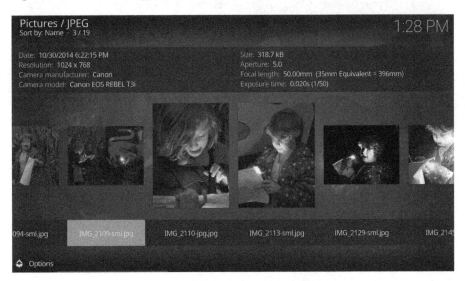

Figure 8-11. *Select a photo to see selected camera and exposure metadata*

■ **Note**   Click the Options button (lower left-hand corner) to change display and playback options for different types of media.

Connecting to a PLEX Server with RasPlex

PLEX servers have become very popular ways to store music and recorded video for use on home networks. So, it's not surprising that Raspberry Pi supports access to the media on a PLEX server with RasPlex.

Although RasPlex is based on Kodi, its user interface is quite different from LibreELEC or most other Kodi-derived media players. RasPlex is optimized for use with a remote control or a keyboard (in its default full-screen mode, mice are not supported).

■ **Tip**   The Flirc USB (flirc.tv) enables standard IR remote controls to work with a Raspberry Pi or other computer being used as a media center. If your HDTV supports CEC, you can control it with RasPlex. See `https://forums.plex.tv/discussion/69014/remote-for-rasplex` and `https://github.com/RasPlex/RasPlex/wiki/Remote-Controls` for details.

Here's how to connect to a PLEX server with RasPlex. In the following example, we use up, down, left, and right arrow and Enter keys on the keyboard.

1. From the Welcome screen, highlight **Next** and press Enter on your keyboard or remote.

2. If your Raspberry Pi is not connected to a network and has a wireless adapter, select a wireless network when prompted. Enter the encryption key and select **Next** to continue.

3. Samba is already enabled, and you can also enable SSH. Select **Next** to continue.

4. If the RasPlex display does not properly fill the screen, select Do Calibrate. Otherwise, select **Next**.

5. To log into your MyPlex account (and log into your local PLEX server), select **Sign in to Plex** when prompted.

6. You can log in by entering the PIN displayed in RasPlex on a computer connected to plex.tv/pin, or highlight Manual and enter your username and password.

7. Select **OK** to complete signin.

8. To improve performance, select Start precaching and select either your local server or the plex.tv server.

9. When image precaching is complete, select Next.

Select your favorite media type, and then choose from available items on the Plex server (Figure 8-12).

Figure 8-12. *Scroll up and down to select a media type, and then to the right to select what to play*

To change settings, press the left arrow key from the home dialog shown in Figure 8-12. This displays a menu with options for changing channel settings, system settings, network connections, and other options (Figure 8-13).

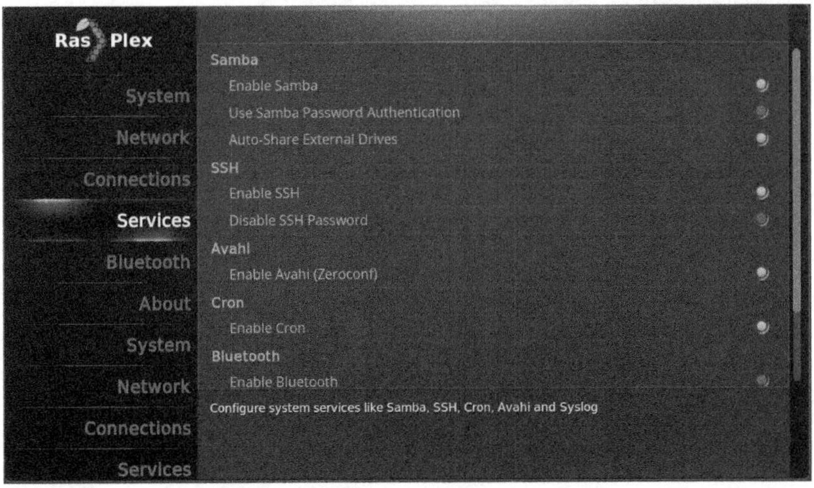

Figure 8-13. *Changing services in RasPlex*

Troubleshooting

Check the following if you have problems with setup, configuration, or media playback:

Network Settings

- You don't need to set up a wireless network in advance. However, if you prefer to use a wired network, connect your Ethernet cable before you start the configuration process.

- If you are unable to log into a network share, go to that computer or device and make sure you are using a username that is already set up on that computer or device along with the correct password.

Audio Playback

- If an HDMI connection is being used with any media playback app, the default is to send audio and video to the HDMI display. If the display is a computer monitor with no speakers, you won't hear anything. Use the configuration settings in the distro to redirect audio to the correct playback device.

Summary

- There are many media-centric Linux distros available for the Raspberry Pi. Many are based on the Kodi distros for Intel x86 and x64 processors.

- BerryBoot and a WD PiDrive make setting up a media server and storing a large amount of media easy.

- LibreELEC supports playback of movies, TV shows, music, music videos, live TV radio, pictures, and videos. Media can be stored on the Raspberry Pi or a network location.

- RasPlex connects to an existing PLEX server for media playback.

CHAPTER 9

■ ■ ■

GPIO Anatomy and Applications

GPIO stands for General-Purpose Input/Output. GPIO pins don't have fixed assignments, so under program control, they can perform many different tasks. In this chapter, you learn the specifics of the GPIO interface and are introduced to programs that can control devices connected to GPIO pins.

All Raspberry Pi models have GPIO connectors; all except the Pi Zero and Pi Zero W have pin headers that make connections very simple. The Pi Zero and Pi Zero W have open holes that can be used for soldered-in-place GPIO interfaces.

Hardware Used in This Chapter

- Raspberry Pi Model B

- Raspberry Pi 2

- Raspberry Pi 3

- Gertboard

- PiFace

- SunFounder kit

What Can You Do with GPIO?

The number of tasks that can be performed by a Raspberry Pi through its GPIO pins is almost unlimited. Here are a few examples:

- Camera control

- Motor control

- Weather monitoring

- Control lights, sounds

© Mark Edward Soper 2017
M. E. Soper, *Expanding Your Raspberry Pi*, DOI 10.1007/978-1-4842-2922-4_9

- Interface and monitor devices
- Run Pi without a full-size display

GPIO Pinouts

Although the 26-pin header on the Raspberry Pi Model A and B and the 40-pin header on the A+, B+, Pi 2, and Pi 3 are commonly referred to as the GPIO header, the header also includes leads for 3.3V and 5V DC power, several ground lines, and three specialized types of data leads:

- UART
- I2C
- SPI

Pins that do not fall into one of the preceding categories can be used in a variety of ways under program control. These pins can also be used for GPIO applications if they are not being used for their specialized tasks.

UART

Universal Asynchronous Receive/Transmit pins can be used for serial (one bit at a time) data transmission and receiving. The UART can be used to control GPIO pins or to monitor boot messages transmitted (by default) by the Linux kernel.

I2C

Inter Integrated Circuit pins are often used to communicate with external boards, such as accelerometers like the Adafruit ADXL345.

SPI

Serial Port Interface pins can be used to connect to multiple devices on the same port. Each device is assigned a separate chip select pin.

Figure 9-1 illustrates the default GPIO pinouts for most Raspberry Pi models. Pi 1 Model A and Model B include a 26-pin connection, while other models include a 40-pin connector.

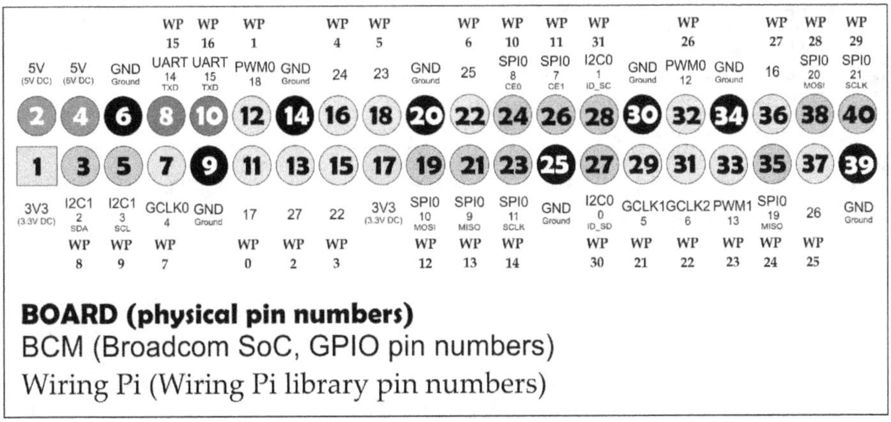

	WP 15	WP 16	WP 1		WP 4	WP 5		WP 6	WP 10	WP 11	WP 31		WP 26		WP 27	WP 28	WP 29
5V (5V DC)	5V (6V DC)	GND Ground	UART 14 TXD	UART 15 TXD	PWM0 18	GND Ground	24	23	GND Ground	25	SPIO 8 CE0	SPIO 7 CE1	I2CO 1 ID_SC	GND Ground	PWM0 12	GND Ground	16	SPIO 20 MOSI	SPIO 21 SCLK

② ④ ⑥ ⑧ ⑩ ⑫ ⑭ ⑯ ⑱ ⑳ ㉒ ㉔ ㉖ ㉘ ㉚ ㉜ ㉞ ㊱ ㊳ ㊵

① ③ ⑤ ⑦ ⑨ ⑪ ⑬ ⑮ ⑰ ⑲ ㉑ ㉓ ㉕ ㉗ ㉙ ㉛ ㉝ ㉟ ㊲ ㊴

3V3 (3.3V DC)	I2C1 2 SDA	I2C1 3 SCL	GCLK0 4	GND Ground	17	27	22	3V3 (3.3V DC)	SPIO 10 MOSI	SPIO 9 MISO	SPIO 11 SCLK	GND Ground	I2CO 0 ID_SD	GCLK1 5	GCLK2 6	PWM1 13	SPIO 19 MISO	26	GND Ground
	WP 8	WP 9	WP 7		WP 0	WP 2	WP 3		WP 12	WP 13	WP 14		WP 30	WP 21	WP 22	WP 23	WP 24	WP 25	

BOARD (physical pin numbers)
BCM (Broadcom SoC, GPIO pin numbers)
Wiring Pi (Wiring Pi library pin numbers)

Figure 9-1. *The default GPIO pin assignments for Raspberry Pi for BOARD, BCM, and wiringPi numbering schemes*

■ **Caution** Revision 1 Pi 1 Models A and B have different default pin assignments. Also, with any version of Raspberry Pi, many pins have alternative uses. For an interactive visual guide to the Raspberry Pi pinout and its variations, visit https://pinout.xyz.

Raspberry Pi GPIO Pin Numbering Schemes

Programs that run on the Raspberry Pi can use any of the following numbering schemes to use particular pins on the PI's GPIO interface (refer to Figure 9-1):

- BOARD
- BCM
- wiringPi

BOARD

The BOARD numbering scheme identifies pins by their physical pin numbers. A Python program that uses the BOARD numbering scheme includes the following code at the start of the program:

```
Import RPi.GPIO as GPIO
GPIO.setmode(GPIO.BOARD)
```

The first line imports the RPi.GPIO library, a program module that enables the program to control GPIO channels. The second line specifies that the program uses the BOARD method. The BOARD method is recommended when you are writing a program that might run on various versions of the Raspberry Pi.

░ **Tip**   For many more details about referring to GPIO pins in Python programs, see
`https://sourceforge.net/p/raspberry-gpio-python/wiki/BasicUsage/`.

BCM

The BCM numbering scheme (also known as the GPIO numbering scheme) identifies pins by the channels used by the Broadcom SoC (system on a chip) processor used on the Raspberry Pi board. A Python program that uses the BCM numbering scheme includes the following code at the start of the program:

```
Import RPi.GPIO as GPIO
GPIO.setmode(GPIO.BCM)
```

The first line imports the RPi.GPIO library. The second line specifies that the program uses the BCM method. The BCM method is very popular, but a program that uses the BCM method won't run on different revisions of the Raspberry Pi unless the program checks for the board version and has different commands for pins that vary between versions.

░ **Note**   Revision 2 Raspberry Pi boards with a 26-pin GPIO header also have a P5 GPIO connector that is designed for an optional header normally soldered to the underside of the board. The mounting holes are next to the 26-pin connector. To see the pinout for this connector, see the P5 header figure at `http://wiringpi.com/pins/`.

---

wiringPi

The wiringPi numbering scheme was adapted from the Wiring pin numbering scheme used by the Arduino microcontroller board (`www.arduino.cc`). Unlike BCM, wiringPi enables programmers to address logical, rather than physical, pins. In practice, this means that programs written using wiringPi won't fail when run on differing revisions of Raspberry Pi.

wiringPi uses the C programming language (`www.wiringpi.com`), but it has been adapted for use on Python, Perl, and PHP. To download a version of wiringPi for these languages, see `https://github.com/WiringPi`. Any Python program that uses wiringPi must include import `wiringpi`, followed by additional statements that configure the pin numbering method used. For additional code snippets and tips, see `https://github.com/WiringPi/WiringPi-Python`.

Programming the GPIO Interface

Originally, the C programming language was used to control devices that plugged into the GPIO connector. The first version of the Gertboard (see "Using a Gertboard" in this chapter) included only C language examples, and wiringPi is a library for the C language. However, Python has become a popular choice for educational uses, so many vendors of add-on devices for Raspberry Pi now provide both C and Python sample programs. The program examples in the remainder of this chapter use Python.

Using a Gertboard

The Gertboard (Figure 9-2) includes an Atmel ATmegs 328p AVR microcontroller, relays, digital/analog and analog/digital converters, an LED light array, and open-collector outputs for use with lamps and relays. With its many different types of connectors, it's a versatile experimentation device. However, the software samples provided with the documentation are designed for the 26-pin Raspberry Pi A and B versions. Due to differences in pinouts and memory locations in later versions of the Raspberry Pi, the Gertboard is not as suitable a choice as newer boards, such as the PiFace Digital (www.piface.org.uk/).

Figure 9-2. *The Gertboard mounted on a Raspberry Pi 1 Model B*

The Gertboard has a 26-pin connector on its underside that mounts to the 26-pin GPIO connector on the top of the Raspberry Pi (Figure 9-3).

173

Figure 9-3. *The Gertboard's connector compared to the GPIO pins on the Raspberry Pi Model B*

The Gertboard is designed for a wide variety of experiments, all of which require the user to connect jumper blocks or wires to various connectors on the Gertboard. The original Gertboard documentation included only C language examples, but the version 2.0 documentation revision included with later production and also online at `www.element14.com/community/docs/DOC-51727/l/assembled-gertboard-user-manual-with-schematics` (free membership required) also includes Python versions of most examples.

■ **Tip**   The easiest way to use examples for the Gertboard or any other add-on for Raspberry Pi is to download and install the language libraries and examples to a system running Raspbian with PIXEL or another GUI, open the example file in a file manager and run it, and then modify it as desired. You can download the Python version of the software and examples for the Gertboard from `http://raspi.tv/downloads`. The Gertboard examples include versions for the GPIO and wiringPi libraries.

Figure 9-4 shows the Gertboard configured for the LEDs program (C version: leds. Python with GPIO numbering: leds-rg.py. Python with wiringPi numbering: leds-wp.py). When you run either Python version, the program displays the correct jumper block/wiring positions before starting (Figure 9-5).

Figure 9-4. *The Gertboard running the LEDs test*

```
pi@raspberrypi:~/gertboard/GB_Python $ sudo python leds-rg.py
These are the connections for the Gertboard LEDs test:
jumpers in every out location (U3-out-B1, U3-out-B2, etc)
GP25 in J2 --- B1 in J3
GP24 in J2 --- B2 in J3
GP23 in J2 --- B3 in J3
GP22 in J2 --- B4 in J3
GP21 in J2 --- B5 in J3
GP18 in J2 --- B6 in J3
GP17 in J2 --- B7 in J3
GP11 in J2 --- B8 in J3
GP10 in J2 --- B9 in J3
GP9 in J2 --- B10 in J3
GP8 in J2 --- B11 in J3
GP7 in J2 --- B12 in J3
(If you don't have enough straps and jumpers you can install
just a few of them, then run again later with the next batch.)
When ready hit enter.

-
```

Figure 9-5. *Running the GPIO version of the LEDs program for Python*

Using a PiFace Control and Display Board

The PiFace Control and Display (PiFace C and D) board was made for the original 26-pin
Raspberry Pi 1 Models A and B, but it also works with the newer versions. The PiFace
Control and Display 2 board is more suited for use with newer models, as it has been
redesigned to avoid being blocked by the additional USB ports on the Pi B+, Pi 2, and Pi 3
boards. However, this author was able to successfully connect the original model to a Pi 2.

As the name implies, the PiFace Control and Display board provides an alternative to a full-size display and keyboard interface. It uses a two-line scrollable LCD display with adjustable contrast. It has a three-position rocker button on the top of the unit (press in the button for a fourth option) and five pushbuttons below the LCD (Figure 9-6).

Figure 9-6. *The PiFace Control and Display board before being mounted on a Raspberry Pi*

To test the PiFace Control and Display board, you can use simple commands that can be run from the Python shell. Figure 9-7 illustrates the commands needed to display the classic "Hello, World!" message. Note that you can program the PiFace C and D board to run with or without the backlight.

```
Python 3.4.2 Shell                                          _ □ ✗

File  Edit  Shell  Debug  Options  Windows  Help

Python 3.4.2 (default, Oct 19 2014, 13:31:11)
[GCC 4.9.1] on linux
Type "copyright", "credits" or "license()" for more information.
>>> import pifacecad
>>> cad = pifacecad.PiFaceCAD()      # create PiFace Control and Display object
>>> cad.lcd.backlight_on()           # turns the backlight on
>>> cad.lcd.write("Hello, world!")   # writes hello world on to the LCD
>>>
                                                          Ln: 8 Col: 4
```

Figure 9-7. *Testing the PiFace Control and Display board with commands from the Python shell*

The sample programs provided by the PiFace web site and manual take full advantage of the interactive nature of the PiFace C and D and its ability to display custom bitmaps. Figure 9-8 illustrates the author editing the word list in the Hangman sample program, while Figure 9-9 illustrates how the PiFace C and D displays the game in progress.

Figure 9-8. Editing the Hangman sample program

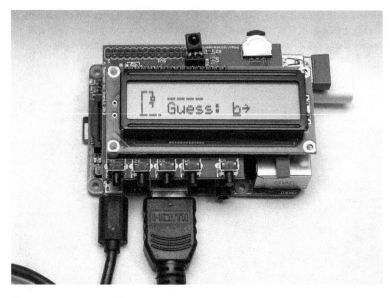

Figure 9-9. *Running the Hangman program*

Using a Breadboard

One of the most flexible ways to experiment with the Raspberry Pi's GPIO pins is to connect jumper wires between the Pi and a device, such as an LED, resistor, or a motor. You can accomplish the same result more easily if you attach a device known as a breadboard to a Raspberry Pi's GPIO pins.

A breadboard (Figure 9-10) has multiple holes for carrying signals between the Raspberry Pi and devices such as resistors, LEDs, motors, small LCD displays, and more. The breadboard illustrated in Figure 9-10 is from the SunFounder Raspberry Pi Super Kit 2.0, which includes a GPIO extension board (breakout board) and ribbon cable that permit the breadboard to be connected in a variety of ways to the Raspberry Pi. This particular kit also includes many jumper wires, resistors, a motor, switches, control and buffer chips, and many other components for conducting experiments.

■ **Note** Other vendors with somewhat similar kits include Adafruit (www.adafruit.com), CamJam EduKit (www.thepihut.com), Monkmakes (www.monkmakes.com), and CanaKit (www.canakit.com).

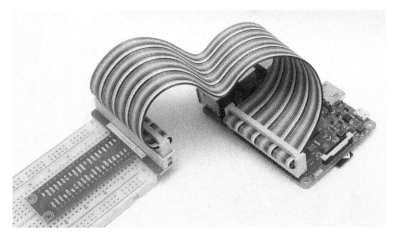

Figure 9-10. *Connecting a breadboard to a Raspberry Pi 2*

■ **Note**   To learn more about the kit shown in Figures 9-10 through 9-12, visit
`www.sunfounder.com/learn/category/Super_Kit_V2_for_RaspberryPi.html`. Tutorials
(including the following sample code) and kit contents are listed there.

In Figure 9-11, the breadboard is connected to power and signal leads that will send
3.3V to a resistor that is connected to an LED. When the following sample program is run, the
LED lights up, then turns off. The pattern repeats until the user kills the program with Ctrl-C.
This program (provided by SunFounder) addresses the GPIO pins using the BOARD method.

```
#!/usr/bin/env python
import RPi.GPIO as GPIO
import time

LedPin = 11    # pin11

def setup():
        GPIO.setmode(GPIO.BOARD)        # Numbers GPIOs by physical location
        GPIO.setup(LedPin, GPIO.OUT)    # Set LedPin's mode is output
        GPIO.output(LedPin, GPIO.HIGH) # Set LedPin high(+3.3V) to off led

def loop():
        while True:
                print '...led on'
                GPIO.output(LedPin, GPIO.LOW)  # led on
                time.sleep(0.5)
                print 'led off...'
                GPIO.output(LedPin, GPIO.HIGH) # led off
                time.sleep(0.5)
```

```
def destroy():
        GPIO.output(LedPin, GPIO.HIGH)      # led off
        GPIO.cleanup()                      # Release resource

if __name__ == '__main__':      # Program start from here
        setup()
        try:
                loop()
        except KeyboardInterrupt:  # When 'Ctrl+C' is pressed, the child
        program destroy() will be  executed.
                destroy()
```

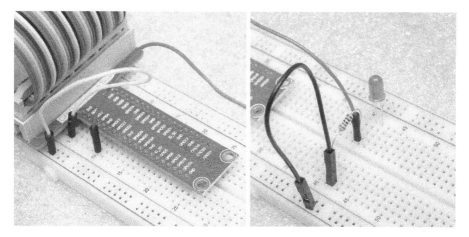

Figure 9-11. *The SunFounder breadboard*

In Figure 9-12, the T-connector is located at the other end of the breadboard and is used to connect to a motor (with propeller) and an external power supply. A controller chip connected to the breadboard provides control signals to the motor.

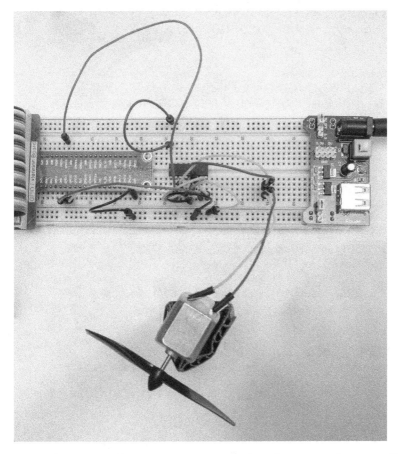

Figure 9-12. *Controlling a motor requires an external power supply, a controller chip, and many additional patch cables compared to the LED light setup in Figure 9-11*

Here's the Python program provided by SunFounder for the setup shown in Figure 9-12:

```
#!/usr/bin/env python
import RPi.GPIO as GPIO
import time


MotorPin1   = 11    # pin11
MotorPin2   = 12    # pin12
MotorEnable = 13    # pin13

def setup():
        GPIO.setmode(GPIO.BOARD)            # Numbers GPIOs by physical location
        GPIO.setup(MotorPin1, GPIO.OUT)  # mode --- output
        GPIO.setup(MotorPin2, GPIO.OUT)
```

```
        GPIO.setup(MotorEnable, GPIO.OUT)
        GPIO.output(MotorEnable, GPIO.LOW) # motor stop

def loop():
    while True:
            print 'Press Ctrl+C to end the program...'
            GPIO.output(MotorEnable, GPIO.HIGH) # motor driver enable
            GPIO.output(MotorPin1, GPIO.HIGH)   # clockwise
            GPIO.output(MotorPin2, GPIO.LOW)
            time.sleep(5)

            GPIO.output(MotorEnable, GPIO.LOW) # motor stop
            time.sleep(5)

            GPIO.output(MotorEnable, GPIO.HIGH) # motor driver enable
            GPIO.output(MotorPin1, GPIO.LOW)     # anticlockwise
            GPIO.output(MotorPin2, GPIO.HIGH)
            time.sleep(5)

            GPIO.output(MotorEnable, GPIO.LOW) # motor stop
            time.sleep(5)

def destroy():
        GPIO.output(MotorEnable, GPIO.LOW) # motor stop
        GPIO.cleanup()                         # Release resource

if __name__ == '__main__':      # Program start from here
        setup()
        try:
                loop()
        except KeyboardInterrupt: # When 'Ctrl+C' is pressed, the child
        program destroy() will be  executed.
                destroy()
```

Regardless of the kit you select, it's very important to visit the vendor's web site:

- You can download and copy program code rather than typing it in yourself

- You may get updated figures to make experiments easier to set up, perform, and modify

In the case of the SunFounder kit, the printed version of the manual showed direct connections between the Pi's GPIO pins and the breadboard using individual patch wires. However, the web site provides a download that includes updated illustrations that showed how to use the ribbon cable and breakout connector to simplify setups.

> ■ **Note** SunFounder and other vendors are using the free and open source
> Fritzing program to create diagrams of their setups. To learn more about Fritzing,
> see `http://fritzing.org/home/`.

Troubleshooting

If you are unable to use a device that connects to the GPIO pins on your Raspberry Pi,
check the following:

- Have you installed the wiring libraries (BCM or wiringPi) needed?
  If the libraries are not installed, the program will crash.

- If your experiment uses the I2C pins on the Raspberry Pi, are they
  enabled? Enable them using raspi-config. For more information,
  see `www.raspberrypi-spy.co.uk/2014/11/enabling-the-i2c-
  interface-on-the-raspberry-pi/`.

- Are you running Python (or other language) as superuser (root)?

- Check the jumper blocks or cables on your Gertboard or
  breadboard.

- If you need to use an external power supply, make sure it is
  configured for the correct voltage level. For example, in the motor
  experiment, 5V DC was needed.

- If you use a resistor, make sure it is the correct rating.

- If you use a LED lamp, make sure it is connected correctly.

Before you turn on the power, look over everything carefully. Incorrect power
connections could fry your experimental devices or your Pi itself.

Summary

- The original versions of the Raspberry Pi (Model A and Model B)
  have 26-pin GPIO pins, while all newer versions have 40-pin GPIO
  pins or open solder holes (Pi Zero and Pi Zero W).

- GPIO (General-Purpose Input/Output) pins can be programmed
  to perform many different tasks.

- Some GPIO pins have primary roles as UART (serial), I2C (inter
  integrated circuit), and SPI (multiple device serial port), but these
  pins can also be reassigned through program control.

- The BOARD pin numbering scheme identifies GPIO pins by their
  physical pin locations.

- The BCM (GPIO) pin numbering scheme identifies GPIO pins by the channels used by the Broadcom SoC chips that power various Raspberry Pi boards.

- The wiringPi pin numbering scheme is based on the Wiring pin numbering scheme used by the Arduino microcontroller board.

- The Gertboard includes an Atmel ATmegs 328p AVR microcontroller, relays, digital/analog and analog/digital converters, an LED light array, and open-collector outputs for use with lamps and relays. It is designed for use with the original Raspberry Pi models with the 26-pin GPIO pinout.

- The PiFace Control and Display board is available in versions for the 26-pin and current 40-pin GPIO pinout. It includes a two-line scrollable LCD display with a rocker/push button and five pushbuttons.

- A breadboard connects to the GPIO pins by means of a ribbon cable and a breakout board. Because the breadboard has the same signals as the GPIO pins, it makes creating circuits easier than connecting directly to the GPIO pins.

CHAPTER 10

▓ ▓ ▓

Taking Your Raspberry Pi on the Road

When you move your Raspberry Pi from the comfort of your home or office into a mobile environment, you're faced with three questions:

- How much power does it use?

- Can I control how much power it uses?

- What can I use for an alternative power source?

In this chapter we'll review all three of these questions. Let's start with power usage.

Power Usage

The model of Raspberry Pi you use and the accessories you use have a huge impact on power usage. If you are planning to use battery power, knowing how much power your Raspberry PI uses is vital to know before you purchase a battery power source.

According to the Raspi.TV's Raspberry Pi 2 – Power and Performance Measurement web site (http://raspi.tv/2015/raspberry-pi2-power-and-performance-measurement), the Raspberry Pi 2 is far more economical when running at idle, loading the LXDE GUI, watching a full HD (1080p) video, and recording a 1080p video than the Pi Model B, and uses only slightly more power than its immediate predecessor, the Pi B+. However, when multicore apps are run, the current draw increases from 280mA (one core) to 420mA (four cores).

Test results at idle on Jeff Geerling's Raspberry Pi Dramble page (www.pidramble.com/wiki/benchmarks/power-consumption) is the source for the graph shown in Figure 10-1. All of these test results were measured after Geerling disabled onboard HDMI and the activity LEDs on each Pi model.

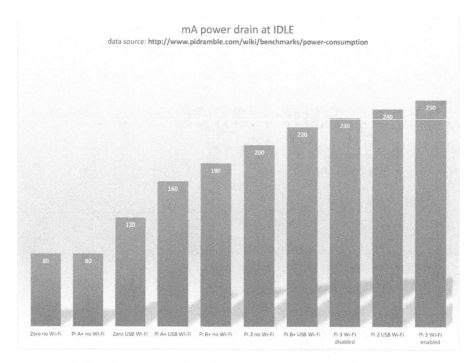

Figure 10-1. *Enabling Wi-Fi (Pi 3) or using a USB Wi-Fi adapter (other models) increases power consumption, but the built-in Wi-Fi in Pi 3 (also used in Pi Zero, not shown) uses only about half the power at idle of a USB Wi-Fi adapter*

Configuring the Raspberry Pi for Minimal Power Consumption

As you learned from the previous section, the amount of power a Raspberry Pi consumes can be adjusted by changing its configuration. If you're accustomed to configuring a PC or MacOS computer, though, tweaking a Pi is a completely different story. Instead of power management in the system firmware (BIOS or UEFI) or operating system dialogs, the Pi uses commands issued from the terminal (command line) or inserted into the startup procedure.

Another difference is that Pi power consumption involves disabling ports and devices, and because of how the Pi is designed internally, disabling a port or onboard device can disable more than you expected.

Disabling HDMI

If you are using a Raspberry Pi in a headless configuration (using a remote device to control it), turning off the HDMI port is a no-pain way to save power (about 25mA). Per Jeff Geerling, you can disable HDMI in two ways. From the command line (Raspbian or similar Linux distros):

/usr/bin/tvservice -o

To disable HDMI at boot, edit /etc/rc.local and add

/usr/bin/tvservice -o

To reenable HDMI from the command line:

/usr/bin/tvservice -p

Disabling Onboard LEDs

Individual LEDs can be disabled from the command line (see https://www.jeffgeerling.com/blogs/jeff-geerling/controlling-pwr-act-leds-raspberry-pi). For Raspberry Pi 2, B+, and A+, run **sudo nano /boot/config.txt** and add these commands to disable both LEDs at boot:

```
# Disable the ACT LED.
dtparam=act_led_trigger=none
dtparam=act_led_activelow=off

# Disable the PWR LED.
dtparam=pwr_led_trigger=none
dtparam=pwr_led_activelow=off
```

Save changes, exit, and reboot.

With Raspberry Pi Zero, there's only one LED to disable. It can be disabled from the command line, or at boot time. Run sudo nano /boot/config.txt and add these commands:

```
# Disable the ACT LED on the Pi Zero.
dtparam=act_led_trigger=none
dtparam=act_led_activelow=on
```

The LEDs on the Raspberry Pi 3 appear to have different default behaviors depending upon the specific Linux distro used. For details, see the discussion thread at www.jeffgeerling.com/blogs/jeff-geerling/controlling-pwr-act-leds-raspberry-pi.

Enabling Login and Control via TTY

Disabling USB ports on the B+, Pi 2, and Pi 3 reduces power consumption significantly, increasing runtime by several hours when using the Pi for periodic photo captures. Unfortunately, these models implement their UBS ports though a hub that also controls the Ethernet port (see https://babaawesam.com/2014/01/24/power-saving-tips-for-raspberry-pi/). Consequently, these steps must be performed before you can boot your system without USB/Ethernet support:

1. Enable Serial with raspi-config or the equivalent in Raspbian with PIXEL or other GUIs

2. Connect a USB to TTL cable (Figure 10-2) from your PC or MacOS computer's USB port to the appropriate pins on the GPIO bus:

   - Green: connect to RXD (receive) pin - PIN 10 (physical)/ GPIO 14

   - White: connect to TXD (transmit) pin - PIN 8 (physical) / GPIO 15

   - Black: connect to GND (ground) pin - PIN 6 or 14 (physical)

   - Red: connect to 5V power pin - PIN 2 or 4 (physical) **only if the Micro-USB power cable is NOT connected to the Raspberry Pi** (see inset in Figure 10-2)

Figure 10-2. *A USB-to-TTL (debug) cable enables you to connect to your Raspberry Pi's GPIO pins for remote control via TTY. The inset (lower right) shows the use of the red power cable in place of the normal Micro-USB power connector on the Raspberry Pi.*

3. Install the appropriate driver for your USB to TTY cable on your PC or MacOS computer. Older cables use the Prolific 2303 chipset driver, while newer cables use the SiLabs CP210X chipset. If you are not certain which cable you use, install both. Most Linux distros already have the appropriate driver installed.

4. You can connect directly to your Raspberry Pi from MacOS's terminal with one of these commands (depending upon the cable's chipset):

   ```
   screen /dev/cu.PL2303* 115200
   ```

   OR

   ```
   screen /dev/cu.usbserial 115200
   ```

5. To connect from another Linux computer, use

   ```
   sudo screen /dev/ttyUSB0 115200
   ```

6. To connect from Windows, download and install PuTTY (`www.chiark.greenend.org.uk/~sgtatham/putty/latest.html`):

   a. Use Windows Device Manager to determine the COM port used by the USB-TTL cable.

   b. Use the Serial Line connection option in PuTTY, specifying the COM port used by the cable and the speed of 115200 (Figure 10-3).

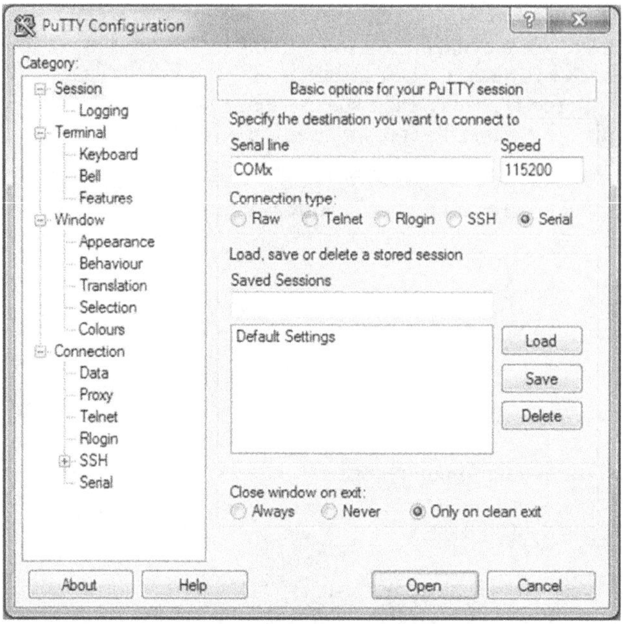

Figure 10-3. *Connecting to the Raspberry Pi with PuTTY. Replace COMX with the actual COM port number as reported by Windows Device Manager.*

7. Log into your Raspberry Pi when prompted.

■ **Tip**   These steps are adapted from the detailed discussion for MacOS, Windows, and Linux connections at `https://learn.adafruit.com/adafruits-raspberry-pi-lesson-5-using-a-console-cable?view=all`. That page also contains illustrations and driver links.

Disabling USB Hub and Ethernet

After booting and logging into your Raspberry Pi via TTL, use the following commands to disable the USB hub which also controls Ethernet:

```
#!/bin/bash
#Code to stop
/etc/init.d/networking stop
echo 0 > /sys/devices/platform/bcm2708_usb/buspower;
echo "Bus power stopping"
```

```
#!/bin/bash
#Code to start
echo 1 > /sys/devices/platform/bcm2708_usb/buspower;
echo "Bus power starting"
sleep 2;
/etc/init.d/networking start
```

If this script does not work, see https://babaawesam.com/2014/01/24/power-saving-tips-for-raspberry-pi/ for a workaround.

Choosing a Power Source

If you want to take your Pi "on the road," you have two choices:

- Battery power

- 12V AC car adapter

Battery power enables you to use your Pi anywhere as long as the battery holds out. A 12V AC car adapter lets you use your Pi on a long car trip. In the following sections, you learn how to make the best choice for your needs.

Estimated Battery Runtimes

You don't need to reduce power consumption before looking at alternative power sources for your Raspberry Pi, but if you decide to use a battery, the combination of larger battery size (measured in mAh) and reduced power drain provides longer runtime.

What level of runtime can you expect? The Spell Foundry Raspberry Pi Battery Life Calculator web site (http://spellfoundry.com/raspberry-pi-battery-runtime-calculator/) provides typical estimated runtimes for standard RPi models in different configurations:

- Selected Pi model

- Pi with USB Wi-Fi adapter

- Pi with Pi Camera

- Pi with USB Wi-Fi adapter and Pi Camera

You might be surprised to discover that using the standard 5MP or 8MP Raspberry Pi camera has a much larger impact on battery life than using a USB Wi-Fi adapter. Figure 10-4 illustrates estimated runtimes based on a standard 2000mAh battery for four current Raspberry Pi models:

- Pi Zero

- Pi A+

- Pi 2

- Pi 3

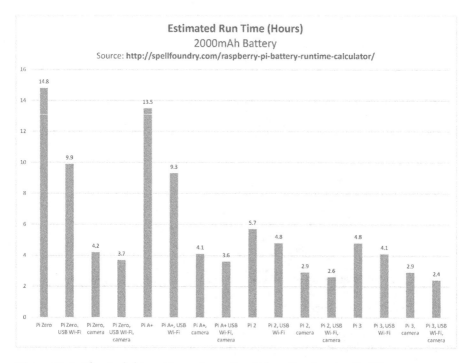

Figure 10-4. *The single biggest impact on estimated runtime is using the Pi's camera*

Figure 10-5 illustrates estimated runtimes for the same models based on a 4000mAh battery.

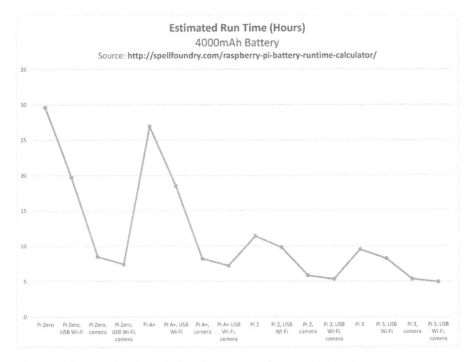

Figure 10-5. *Doubling the mAh (milliampere-hour) rating doubles the runtime*

To increase battery life over these figures, use the tips provided in the section "Configuring the Raspberry Pi for Minimal Power Consumption," in this chapter.

Car Chargers and Raspberry Pi

Car chargers that plug into the 12V auxiliary power jack would seem, at first glance, to be the perfect power source for a Raspberry Pi that's away from home. Unfortunately, car chargers are not intended to provide the precise voltage levels needed to reliably operate a Raspberry Pi.

For example, a 5V DC charger with a 1A output does not provide nearly enough power for a Raspberry Pi other than a Pi Zero. A 5V DC charger with a 2.1A or higher output has the same rating as the power supplies made for Raspberry Pi 2 and 3. However, poor voltage regulation (such as dropping from 5V to 4.5V under load) can prevent a Raspberry Pi from booting or could cause it to crash after starting.

For recommendations for chargers, see the following:

- www.raspberrypi.org/forums/viewtopic.php?f=26&t=48661
  "Using a mirco [sic] USB car charger with the Raspberry Pi"

- www.buyraspberrypi.com.au/shop/12-volt-to-5-volt-3000ma-
  step-down-transformer/ (similar products are available in other
  markets)

Poor-quality cables that have excessive resistance (typically those made with thin wires) can also prevent your Pi from receiving full power. For recommendations and comparisons, see the following:

- www.raspberrypi.org/forums/viewtopic.php?f=63&t=165393
  "Best Micro-USB cables"

- www.cpmspectrepi.uk/raspberry_pi/MoinMoinExport/
  USBcableResChk.html "USB Hub & PSU Cable Resistance
  Checks"

Using Intelligent Power Management Peripherals

Raspberry Pi computers do not have onboard power management features, and as a consequence cannot detect low battery levels or shut down before battery power is exhausted. When a Raspberry Pi shuts down unexpectedly, the chances of memory card corruption are very high. This can lead to the loss of data stored on the memory card, such as time-lapse photos, videos, network monitoring logs, and so on.

As we learned in Chapter 9, the Pi's GPIO pins can be used for a wide variety of peripherals that add new features. In this section, you learn about a few of the devices that use the GPIO pins to provide the missing pieces of power management.

MoPi Mobile Power for Raspberry Pi

The MoPi mobile power peripheral for Raspberry Pi connects to the first 26 pins of the 40-pin GPIO interface on newer models and also supports the early models that have a 26-pin GPIO interface. MoPi uses the I2C bus, the 5V out pin, and a ground pin. It offers the ability to connect to almost any type of power supply that can produce at least 6.2V DC under load (maximum is 20V DC).

Although it includes two default battery profiles (nonrechargeable or nonbattery; eight NiMH rechargeable batteries) that are jumper-selectable, MoPi includes a configuration utility that is used to select power supply type, number of individual battery cells, and battery chemistry.

The software used by MoPi includes

- `simbamond`: SIMple Battery MONitor daemon (system service)

- `mopi`: Configuration tool similar in appearance to raspi-config

- `mopicli`: Command-line interface (CLI) for mopi

- `monit`: Monitors simbamond and other system statuses

In addition to providing optimized power for the Pi, MoPi can shut down the Pi in a controlled manner before the battery source runs out of power, acts as a UPS when both battery and nonbattery power is available, supports hot-swapping of power supplies, and has an integrated on-off switch. MoPi supports programs in Python.

The current model does not support the Raspberry Pi 3 (but supports the Pi 2 and all other models). An updated version (tentatively named MoPi ++) will support the Pi 3 and is expected by the end of 2017.

To learn more about MoPi, see `https://pi.gate.ac.uk/pages/mopi.html`. To order MoPi, see `https://pi.gate.ac.uk/pages/get-mopi.html`.

LiFePO$_4$wered/Pi 3

The LiFePO$_4$wered/Pi 3 is optimized for extreme portability. Like the MoPi, it uses the I2C bus for communications. However, it uses only the first eight pins of the Pi's header. It is compatible with all 40-pin GPIO Raspberry Pi models. A Pi Zero will need to have an eight-pin header installed. Minor adjustments are needed to run on Model A and Model B.

It includes a 1500mAh lithium iron phosphate (LiFePO) cell that has a nominal output voltage of 3.2V, a smart USB charge controller, autoadjusting for input amperages ranging from 1.33A to 500mA, MPPT (solar cell) compatibility, power management, auto shutdown when battery voltage approaches critical levels, a wake timer, auto boot when sufficient power is restored, and charge and power LEDs.

LiFePO$_4$wered/Pi 3 uses a CLI (command-line interface) tool to change parameters. To learn more about the /Pi 3 and original /Pi versions or to purchase, go to `http://lifepo4wered.com/`.

■ **Note** LiFePO (also known as LFP) batteries, unlike standard lithium-ion batteries, are nonflammable and will not explode. They are designed to work at temperatures above 60 degrees C. Their nominal 3.2V voltage remains the same throughout the discharge cycle. They have a low self-discharge rate, enabling them to stay charged even when stored for a long time and are designed to exceed 1,000 charge/discharge cycles.

Sleepy Pi and Sleepy Pi 2

Sleepy Pi (26-pin Raspberry Pi) and Sleepy Pi 2 (40-pin Raspberry Pi) combines the microcontroller interfacing of an Arduino with a real-time clock and wake-on-demand circuitry, current monitor, and support for battery power ranging from 5.5-30V DC.

Like the other products we've examined, Sleepy Pi/Pi 2 connect via the I2C header pins. However, because Sleepy Pi products also contain the ATMEGA328P chip for Arduino functions, many additional pins are used (see Figure 10-6).

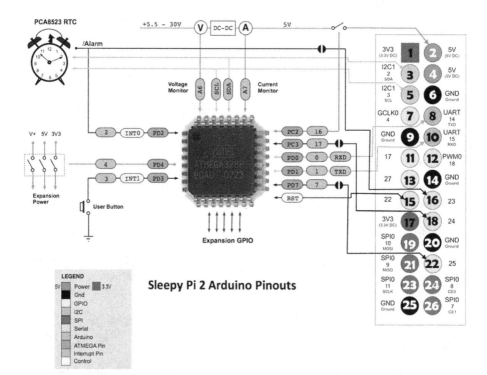

Figure 10-6. *How the Sleepy Pi 2 routes signals between its built-in Arduino chip and the Raspberry Pi's GPIO pins (adapted from a diagram at* http://spellfoundry.com/product/sleepy-pi-2/)

Both products are available in low-profile and stackable versions. The stackable version can be used with other add-on devices. For more information or to order in the EU, see http://spellfoundry.com/products/. To order in the United States and Canada, visit http://buyapi.ca/.

■ **Caution**   The Sleepy Pi/Pi 2 boards have 3.3V (also known as 3V3) GPIO pins, compared to 5V GPIO pins on some Arduino boards. Check GPIO voltages when running an Arduino app on a Sleepy Pi/Pi 2 board.

Comparing Power Management Products for Raspberry Pi

The three products highlighted in the preceding are just some of the power management products made for Raspberry Pi. Whichever products you're interested in, a table such as the following (Table 10-1) can be useful in determining the features you need.

Table 10-1. *Selected Raspberry Pi Add-ons for Power Management Comparison*

Product	Power Source	Power Monitoring	Stackable	RTC	Notes
Sleepy Pi	User-supplied	Yes	Yes*	Yes	Arduino included
LiFePO$_4$wered/ Pi 3	1500mAh LFP battery	Yes	Yes*	No	Smart USB and solar charging
MoPi	User-supplied	Yes	Yes*	No	Very compact

*Specify stackable version when ordering

Troubleshooting

Disabling Raspberry Pi features or connecting devices to your Pi's GPIO pins can be risky if you're careless. To avoid problems, use these guidelines:

- Make a backup copy (clone) of your current OS installation before you experiment. If you make a mistake, you still have your original.

- Be sure to carefully review commands you add to configuration files or run from CLI when configuring your Pi or a peripheral.

- Double-check compatibility before buying or installing a power management device.

- Never install a device to the GPIO pins while the Pi is powered.

- If you are planning to run your Pi from TTY, check TTY login and operation before you disable your HDMI port.

If you have problems after you make configuration changes or connect a peripheral, check the following:

- Make sure you have installed all updates needed for Raspbian.

- Install the latest version of the peripheral's software. Depending upon the peripheral, you might need to install the software before or after connecting the peripheral.

- Check commands and programs for typos.

Summary

Even though the Raspberry Pi was never designed to be "on the road," careful optimization of power requirements, using the largest batteries available, using well-regulated 12V DC car chargers, and power management devices can help the Pi perform as well away from home as in the home, office, or classroom. With many Raspberry Pi models and a variety of approaches to power available, be sure to check compatibility before buying. Use a USB voltage and current tester to verify the quality of power you get from battery or 12V car charger power sources.

Index

A

Adafruit web site, 54
Android devices, 80–81
  RaspiCAM Remote, 138, 140
ApplePi-Baker, 42
Arch Linux ARM, 26

B

Backends, 75, 147
Battery runtimes, 191, 193
BCM numbering scheme, 171–172
BerryBoot
  compatible distros, 157
  configuration, 33
  install, 34
  install distro, 35
  load OS, 38
  more options, 37
  multiboot configuration, 36
  OS, 34–35
  supports, 33
  7-Zip archive file extractor, 158–161
BerryCam, 140, 142
Board-level connectors, 13
BOARD numbering scheme, 171
Breadboard
  multiple holes functions, 178
  SunFounder Raspberry
    Pi Super Kit 2.0, 178
    BOARD method program, 179, 180
    Python program, 181–182
    T-connector, 180–181
Bus-powered USB drives, 53

C

Camera interface (CSI), 13
Cameras
  app issues, 154
  cable, 153
  issues, 153
  5MP version, 124
  8MP version, 124
  port
    connect cable to, 124
    enable, 127–128
    raspi-config, 128
  python, 136, 138
  swap cables for Zero, 125–127
Car chargers, 193–194
CentOS, 39, 46, 47
Common Unix Printing
    System (CUPS)
  add printer, 72–74
  default user group, 72
  install, 72–74
  install printer drivers, 107–108
  log into, 104
  multifunction device, 107
  Print Administration group, 103
  remote administration, 104
  selection process, 105, 107
  troubleshoot, 121
  web browser, 72

D

Display interface (DSI), 13
Dramble Benchmarks page, 44

© Mark Edward Soper 2017
M. E. Soper, *Expanding Your Raspberry Pi*, DOI 10.1007/978-1-4842-2922-4

E

eLinux RPi card, 44
Epson XP-800 multifunction device, 147
Ethernet port and switch
    dnsmasq.conf file, 95
    edit files, 93
    install package, 93
    iptables terms and syntax, 96
    NAT, 95
    ping command, 97
    routing table, 97
    swap ports, 98
    wireless connection, 93–97
EXIF data, 135–136
External hard drive, 53, 59
ext4 file system, 53

F

FAT32 Format, 13, 40–41
Fedora, 39
Flash memory card partitions
    CentOS distros, 46
    current size, 46
    distros and expanded, 45
    existing partition, 50–52
    flash drive (*see* USB flash drive)
    incorrect format, 58
    Linux distros, 46
    parted, 47
    RaspEx, 46
    RISC OS, 48
    root-fs expand, 47
Flirc USB (flirc.tv), 166
FreeBSD, 38
Fswebcam package, 143–144

G

General-Purpose Input/Output (GPIO), 2
    BCM, 172
    BOARD, 171
    breadboard, 178–182
    C programming language, 173
    examples, 169
    Gertboard, 173–175
    I2C, 170
    PiFace Control and Display
        board, 175, 177–178
    Python programming language, 173
    SPI, 170

UART, 170
wiringPi, 172
Gertboard
    components, 173
    connectors, 173–174
    LEDs program, 174–175
Gparted, 51
Guvcview package, 144–145

H

Hangman sample program, 177–178
Headless boot
    connect via SSH, 118, 120
    raspi-config, 118

I, J

I2C
    LiFePO4wered/Pi 3, 195
    MoPi, 194
    sleepy Pi/Pi 2, 196
Image scanner
    SANE, 147–148
    Simple Scan, 148–150
    Xscan, 150–153
Integrated network features, 13–15
Inter integrated circuit (I2C) pins, 170
Internet connection, sharing an
    autoconfiguration address, 98
    check IP address, 98
    encryption key, 89
    Ethernet port and switch, 93–97
    list of packages, 86
    NAT, 89
    network configuration, 87, 89
    Raspbian Jessie, 89–93
    SSID, 89
    troubleshooting, 98
    USB Wi-Fi dongle, 86
    wired connection, 87, 89–93
    wired Ethernet port, 86
    wireless connection, 93–97
Internet of Things (IOT) core, 25
iOS
    BerryCam, 140, 142
    Raspberry Pi, 82–83

K

Kodi media player
    LibreELEC, 161–165
    RasPlex, 166–167

L

Lakka_R Pi 2, 22
LibreELEC
    media files, 163–164, 166
    rename, 162
LibreELEC_R Pi 2, 21
LiFePO$_4$ wered/Pi 3, 195
Linux distros, 45–46
    CentOS, 39
    Fedora, 39
    FreeBSD, 38
    general-purpose compute, 39
    Linux, 42
    NetBSD, 38
    NOOBS
        Lakka_R Pi 2, 22
        LibreELEC_R Pi 2, 21
        OSMC_P2, 23
        RISC OS, 24
        Windows 10 IoT core, 25
    OpenWRT, 39
    PINN
        Arch Linux ARM, 26
        RetroPie, 27
    root-fs expand, 47
    OSX (MacOS), 42
    Windows, 40–41
Linux Samba server configuration
    home folders, 79
    local users, create, 76
    logging, 79–80
    network user, create, 77
    share, 78
    statement, 78
    uncomment statement, 77
Login process, 65

M

MacOS (OSX)
    EXIF data, 136
    PIXEL, 65, 67
    Samba, 113–114
    SANE, 118
Media server
    audio playback, 168
    BerryBoot and WD PiDrive, 158,
        160–161
    BerryBoot-compatible distros, 157
    LibreELEC, 161–164, 166
    network settings, 168
    PLEX servers, 166–167
    RasPlex, 166–167
Memory card
    Dramble Benchmarks page, 44
    eLinux RPi card, 44
    flash (see Flash memory card
        partitions)
    microSD, 43
microSD card, 40, 43–45
Model A family
    features, 3
    Model A+, 3–4
Model B family
    first generation, 5–6
    second generation, 6, 8
    third generation, 6, 8
Monit software, 195
Mopicli software, 195
MoPi mobile power
    battery profiles, 194
    monit, 195
    mopi, 195
    mopicli, 195
    Pi 3, 195
    simbamond, 195
MP4Box, 132–133

N

NetBSD, 38
Network address translation (NAT), 87, 89, 95
Network printer
    CUPS, 72–74
    self-test page, 75
    Set Default Options, 74
Network scanner, 75
New Out of Box Setup (NOOBS)
    install OS, 27–28
    Lakka_R Pi 2, 22
    LibreELEC_R Pi 2, 21
    OSMC_P2, 23
    PINN, 30–31, 33
    restart, 28–30
    RISC OS, 24
    startup options, 29
    Windows 10 IoT core, 25

■ O

OMXplayer, 132
OpenWRT, 39
OSMC_P2, 23
OSX (MacOS), 42

■ P, Q

Parted, 47
Pi 3, 186
Pi Zero W, 10
Picamera
    H.264 video streams, 137
    install, 136
    3.1MP photo, 137
    raspistills, 136
    raspivid, 136
    update, 136
PiDrive BerryBoot Edition, 56
PiDrive Foundation Edition, 55, 57
PiDrive Node Zero, 55, 57–58
PiFace control and display board
    Hangman sample
        program, 177–178
    LCD display, 176
    original model, 175
    testing, 176
PINN
    advanced menu, 31
    Arch Linux ARM, 26
    Clone option, 32–33
    main menu, 31
    NOOBS, 30–31, 33
    RetroPie, 27
PIXEL
    desktop, 17–19
    MacOS (OSX), 65, 67
    Windows share, 61–64
PLEX servers, 166–167
Power
    battery runtimes, 191, 193
    car chargers, 193–194
    disabling HDMI, 187
    disabling onboard LEDs, 187
    enable login, 188–190
    Ethernet, disabling, 190–191
    guidelines, 197
    management comparison, 197
    management features, 194
    supply, 15

    usage, 185
    USB hub, disabling, 190–191
    without USB/Ethernet
        support, 188–189
Print and scan server
    check wireless connection, 101
    connect via USB, 100
    CUPS (*see* Common Unix Printing
        System (CUPS))
    headless boot (*see* Headless boot)
    Samba (*see* Samba)
    SANE (*see* Scanner Access Now Easy
        (SANE))
    select distro, 100
    set up wireless configuration, 102
    troubleshoot, 120
Printed circuit board (PCB), 124
PuTTY, 118, 120

■ R

Raspberry Pi
    common features, 2
    models, 1–2
    ports
        includes, 12
        types and quantities, 12
        Zero models, 12
Raspbian, 17
Raspbian Jessie, 89–93
    Lite, 17, 20, 100–101, 130–131
RaspiCAM Remote, 145–146
    issues, 154
    logging, 138
    setup menu, 139–140
Raspistill
    photo metadata, 135–136
    to take photos, 133–134
    time-lapse photos, 134
Raspivid video capture
    examples, 129–130
    MP4Box, 132–133
    OMXplayer, 132
    options, 129
    Raspbian Jessie Lite, 130, 131
RasPlex, 166–167
RedHat Enterprise, 39
RetroPie, 27
RISC OS, 24, 48
Rootfs-expand, 47

S

Samba
  configuration, 108–109
  install, 108
  Linux server configuration
    home folders, 79
    local users, create, 76
    logging, 79–80
    network user, create, 77
    share, 78
    statement, 78
    uncomment statement, 77
  MacOS (OSX), 113–114
  Windows 7, 109–111
  Windows 8.1, 111–112
  Windows 10, 111–112
SanDisk connect wireless flash drive
  Chromium browser, 69
  IP address, 68–69
  WebDAV supports, 68
Scanner Access Now Easy (SANE)
  available scanners, 115
  backends, 75
  configure, 116
  determine ownership, 116–117
  edit, 116
  install, 115
  issues, 154
  MacOS (OSX), 118
  network scanner, 75
  with PIXEL, 147–148
  rebbot system, 117
  SaneTWAIN, 117
  SANEWinDS, 117
  SwingSANE, 118
  testing, 116
  troubleshoot, 121
  Windows, 117
  xSANE Win32, 118
SD Card Formatter, 40, 42
SDHC memory cards, 13
SDXC memory cards, 13
Seagate wireless plus drive
  supports, 69
  upload content, 71
Serial Port Interface (SPI) pins, 170
Simbamond software, 195
Simple Scan
  configure, 148–149
  save, 150

scan file, 150
select, 149
Sleepy Pi/Pi 2, 196
  3.3V GPIOpins, 196
smbclient, 64
SSH, 118, 120
SSID, 89
SunFounder Raspberry Pi Super Kit 2.0, 179
  BOARD method program, 179–180
  includes, 178
  Python program, 181–182
  T-connector, 180–181
SwingSANE, 118
System-on-a-Chip (SoC)
  BCM, 172
  board, 10
  CPU and RAM, 11
  features, 11

T

Time-lapse photos, 134

U, V

Universal Asynchronous Receive/
    Transmit (UART) pins, 170
USB flash drive
  connection procedure, 48, 50
  existing partition, 50–52
  ext4 file system, 53
  Linux, 48
  read/write access, 50
USB hard drive
  bus-powered, 53
  power supply, 59
  read/write mode, 59

W

WDLabs Pi drive
  3A offers, 57
  BerryBoot edition, 56
  Node Zero, 55, 57–58
  PiDrive Foundation Editions, 55, 57
Webcam
  capture video, 144–145
  check compatibility, 154
  fswebcam, 143–144
  guvcview, 144–145
  RaspiCAM Remote, 145–146

Win32 Disk Imager, 40–41
Windows, 40–41
    share with
        PIXEL, 61–64
        smbclient, 64
Windows 7, 109–110
Windows 8.1, 111–112
Windows 10, 111–112
Windows 10 IoT core, 25
Wired connection
    NAT, 89
    Raspbian Jessie, 89–93
Wireless adapter, 89-93
Wireless drives, 58
WiringPi numbering
        schemes, 171–172

X, Y

xSANE Win32, 118
Xscan
    configure, 150–151
    save, 152
    select, 151

Z

Zero models
    features, 9–10
    ports, 12
    swap cables, 125–127
    v1.2 *vs.* v.1.3, 10
7-Zip, 40

Get the eBook for only \$5!

Why limit yourself?

With most of our titles available in both PDF and ePUB format, you can access your content wherever and however you wish—on your PC, phone, tablet, or reader.

Since you've purchased this print book, we are happy to offer you the eBook for just \$5.

To learn more, go to http://www.apress.com/companion or contact support@apress.com.

Apress®

CPSIA information can be obtained
at www.ICGtesting.com
Printed in the USA
LVHW08s1816190918
590670LV00002B/74/P